# SUGARCRAFT
# FLOWERS

# SUGARCRAFT
# FLOWERS

## 25 step-by-step projects for simple garden flowers

CLAIRE WEBB

NEW HOLLAND

DEDICATION
To Vida, the best leaf maker I know and a very special friend.

This paperback edition first published in 2009
Published in 2006 by New Holland Publishers (UK) Ltd
London · Cape Town · Sydney · Auckland

Garfield House, 86–88 Edgware Road, London, W2 2EA, United Kingdom
www.newhollandpublishers.com

80 McKenzie Street, Cape Town 8001, South Africa
Unit 1, 66 Gibbes Street, Chatswood, NSW 2067, Australia
218 Lake Road, Northcote, Auckland, New Zealand

ISBN 978 1 84773 663 5

Senior Editor: Clare Sayer
Production: Hazel Kirkman
Design: Casebourne Rose Design Associates
Photographer: Shona Wood
Editorial Direction: Rosemary Wilkinson

5 7 9 10 8 6 4

Reproduction by Colourscan, Singapore
Printed and bound by Times Offset (M) Sdn. Bhd., Malaysia

IMPORTANT
None of the flower projects in this book are designed to be eaten – they are for decoration only.
Although flowerpaste and most colourings are edible, all the flowers are created using wire, florist's tape and cotton. Some
dusting powders are non-edible – please check before assembling on any cake. It is a good idea to arrange your flowers in small acrylic stands
to position on cakes or use a posy pick to avoid contamination.

# contents

# introduction

This book contains a collection of 25 beautiful flower projects, all of which can be attempted by complete beginners and experienced sugarcrafters alike. The idea behind the book was to create a collection of simple garden flowers, rather than grand exotic ones, so there are plenty of well loved favourites here, including the delicate primrose, forget-me-not and daisy, as well as the bold and colourful sunflower, anemone and, of course, the rose. I hope that you will be inspired and encouraged to have a go at creating these lovely flowers which are so familiar. Some of the projects are really straightforward while others are a little more challenging, and the range of flowers included covers a variety of techniques.

In sugarcraft, realism is all-important and I have tried to make the flowers as lifelike as possible. Often it is the tiny details that make all the difference. I believe that you get greater satisfaction if what you have made looks natural – I have always found when teaching, the closer to the real thing that was achieved, the happier people were.

I hope that by following these projects you will be inspired to make your own flowers and I'm sure that even experienced sugarcrafters will find plenty of inspiration here too.

# tools and equipment

Before you start making any of the flower projects in this book you will need some essential flower-making equipment, which you will use over and again. The basics are flowerpaste, edible glue, a non-stick board, a small rolling pin, modelling tools, a petal pad, veiners and cutters. The tools and materials needed to make each flower are listed with the individual projects so check what you need before you start. The equipment used in the book is available from good sugarcraft suppliers (see page 79).

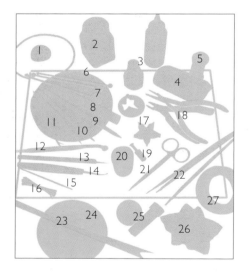

| 1 | spot stand | 15 | cocktail stick |
| 2 | confectioner's glaze | 16 | stamens |
| | | 17 | cutters |
| 3 | edible glues | 18 | wire cutters |
| 4 | flowerpaste | | and pliers |
| 5 | cotton thread | 19 | blossom |
| 6 | petal pad | | plunger cutter |
| 7 | ball tools | 20 | paste colouring |
| 8 | rolling pin | 21 | scissors |
| 9 | Cel stick | 22 | paintbrushes |
| 10 | veining tool | 23 | floral wire |
| 11 | tweezers | 24 | paint palette |
| 12 | cutting wheel | 25 | dusting powder |
| 13 | craft knife | 26 | veiners |
| 14 | dresden tool | 27 | florist's tape |

## Board and rolling pin

You will need a good non-stick board for rolling out flowerpaste. Grooved boards and rolling pins are available but I always prefer to use a plain board and rolling pin as I think you get a more delicate ridge if you create it yourself, which means that your flower or leaf will look less clumsy.

## Petal pad

This is a very useful piece of equipment used for balling and softening leaves and petals. It saves you using the palm of your hand and so stops the flowerpaste from getting sticky.

## Modelling tools

Modelling petals and leaves is a crucial part of making sugarpaste flowers. A ball or dogbone tool is used to cup and soften the edges of leaves and petals, while a dresden tool is used mainly to vein and

hollow out. A craft knife is useful for cutting round templates. Cel sticks are modelling pins that have one rounded end and one pointed end. Cocktail sticks (toothpicks) are also essential if you file one end so it is smooth and rounded.

## Paintbrushes

You will need a small selection of fine good-quality paintbrushes, preferably made from sable, for painting in details. A flat 5-mm (1/4-in) brush is useful for dusting.

## Florist's tape

Florist's tape is used for taping flowers and leaves together. It is available in a range of colours, the most popular being light green, dark green, white, beige and brown. The papery type is by far the best. It comes in a standard width and often a project calls for 'half-' or 'one-third-width' tape. Simply use a pair of scissors to cut the tape lengthways.

## HELPFUL HINTS

✳ Use a small amount of cornflour (cornstarch) on your fingertips if paste is sticking to them.

✳ If your flowerpaste begins to crumble, knead with a little white fat or edible glue.

✳ If your flowerpaste loses its elasticity, knead in a small amount of gum tragacanth, wrap in cling film and leave for about 30 minutes.

## Wires

Floral wires are available in green and white and can be either covered or uncovered. Wire is measured by the Standard Wire Gauge system (SWG or g). The higher the gauge the thinner the wire. I always use white because it doesn't show through the paste and you cover any exposed wire with florist's tape.

## Cutters and veiners

A huge range of cutters is now available for making sugarpaste flowers. These are useful for cutting basic shapes, which you can then form and shape by hand to achieve the desired result. Each project lists the cutters recommended, all of which are available from good sugarcraft suppliers. Veiners can also be bought commercially, but you can achieve very realistic results with a dresden tool or by using real leaves as templates. A ceramic veiner is a small tool that is useful for veining petals.

## Other tools and materials

You will also need the following: tweezers, fine scissors, small round-nosed pliers, wire cutters, plain-edged cutting wheel, assortment of stamens, cotton thread, edible glue, hi-tack (non-toxic) glue, confectioner's glaze, blocks of oasis, cornflour (cornstarch), gum tragacanth and isopropyl alcohol (used to thin down confectioner's glaze).

## Flowerpaste

Ready-made flowerpaste is available in a wide range of colours. It usually comes in packets of 100 g (3$^1$/2 oz) and some colours are available in packets of 200 g (7 oz). You will probably only use flowerpaste in small quantities, so cut off what you need for each flower or leaf and, to ensure the surplus does not dry out, return it to a plastic bag and keep well sealed in an airtight container or wrap with cling film. This stops it from drying out so you can use it again. Some brands of flowerpaste can be frozen and used later so do check the manufacturer's instructions.

## Colouring flowerpaste

Although flowerpaste comes in a wide range of colours, you may want to colour your own to a particular shade. Paste and powder colourings both give excellent results when colouring flowerpaste but I prefer to use paste colours for colouring and dusting powders (petal dust) to add depth of colour or detail to smaller areas. The easiest way to add paste colour to flowerpaste is to dip a cocktail stick (toothpick) into the colour and then onto the flowerpaste. Knead well and add more colour little by little until the desired colour is achieved.

When making very dark flowers and leaves, it is best not to colour the paste too deeply. Keep it three or four shades lighter than you actually need. When the item is dry, you can then dust over it with a deep-coloured dusting powder. The flowers or leaves can then be steamed. If you still want to deepen the colour, allow to dry completely and follow the same process again.

Dusting powders (petal dust) fall into two categories: edible and non-edible. Make sure you are aware of which one you are using.

# basic recipes

Ready-made flowerpaste and edible glues are easily available, but you can make your own by following these simple recipes.

## Materials

454 g (1 lb/3 cups) icing sugar
15 ml (3 tsp) gum tragacanth
25 ml (5 tsp) warm water
10 ml (2 tsp) liquid glucose
15 ml (1 tbsp) white vegetable fat
12 ml (2.5 tsp) powdered gelatin
1 large egg white

## Flowerpaste

**1** Put the icing sugar into a large heatproof bowl. Mix in the gum tragacanth and place in an oven on a very low heat to warm through.

**2** Take another heatproof bowl and add the water, glucose and vegetable fat and mix well. Sprinkle the gelatin all over. Place over a pan of hot water and heat through, stirring occasionally until all the ingredients have dissolved.

**3** Warm the beater of an electric food mixer, add the sugar mix, dissolved ingredients and egg white. With the mixer on its lowest speed, beat until the mixture starts to come away from the sides of the bowl in strings.

**4** Turn the paste onto a board and knead it together into a smooth ball. Place in a polythene bag in an airtight container in the refrigerator. Leave for 24 hours before using.

## Edible glue

In a small, sterilized heatproof jar, place one part gum tragacanth to three/four parts hot water. Stir and replace the lid and leave to dissolve. If the glue is a little too thick add some more water until you are happy with the consistency.

## Gum glue

Break off a small piece of flowerpaste and mash it up with a small amount of edible glue. It will turn into a sort of soft gum consistency. This will make a strong adhesive suitable for assembly of larger items and repairs.

# techniques

The following techniques provide the grounding you need to make a wide variety of sugarcraft flowers. You will find that you use one or more of them for most projects.

## Making flowers

Cutters are used extensively in this book, but it can be useful to learn and practise making flower shapes without them. This practice will give you a feel for the material and sharpen up your sculpting skills.

### Making pulled flowers

This is a basic sugarcraft technique. Pulled or finger flowers are made completely by hand without using cutters. You can use them as fillers in sprays or you can make flowers such as violets and pansies using a variation on the technique.

Before you start you will need to round off one end of a cocktail stick (toothpick) with an emery board. It is also useful to make a similar tool from a piece of wooden dowel for larger flowers.

**1** Break off a small piece of flowerpaste, roll it into a ball, then form it into a teardrop shape.

**2** Push the rounded end of the cocktail stick (toothpick) into the pointed end of the teardrop to open it up a little.

**3** Make small cuts downwards according to how many petals you require.

**4** Form the petals either by squeezing the tip between your thumb and index finger or by rolling with a cocktail stick (toothpick). Work the paste until the correct petal shape is formed.

## Making violets

**1** Follow steps 1-2 of Making Pulled Flowers, left, only this time hollow out the cone, making sure the edges are thin. Make five fairly deep cuts to represent petals; four should be the same size, the other one larger. Cut off the points on the corners of the petals with a fine pair of scissors.

**2** Place the petals in turn on your index finger and roll with a cocktail stick (toothpick) to widen and slightly lengthen them. Make sure the bottom petal stays larger than the others. Carefully push the two top petals backwards, the middle two a little inwards and bring the larger bottom one forwards.

**3** Redefine the spur at the back of the flower by rolling it between your thumb and index finger, giving it a gentle curve upwards. Place a small stamen (normally orange for a violet) in the throat of the flower. Insert a length of 28-gauge wire with a hooked end that has been moistened with edible glue behind the top two petals. Leave to dry.

## Making flowers using the Mexican hat method

**1** Take a small piece of flowerpaste and form it into a cone. Pinch out the paste from the thick end, leaving a centre post (it should resemble a Mexican hat). Roll out from the centre to thin down.

**2** This technique does make use of cutters. Place your chosen cutter over the post and cut out the shape you require.

**3** If the post is too thick, dust your fingertips with cornflour (cornstarch) and pick up the shape. Place the post between your index finger and thumb and twist to narrow it. Insert a wire into the end of the post.

13

## Making leaves

The techniques used to make leaves and single petals are exactly the same. Leaves are a very important part of any floral work, without realistic foliage the flowers lose their realism. First choose a colour that matches the plant most closely. For green leaves I use green flowerpaste dusted with a selection of dusting powders (petal dust). Brown leaves are made from cream flowerpaste, then dusted as before.

### Basic leaves and petals

**1** Roll out a piece of flowerpaste quite thinly, leaving a narrow ridge of thicker paste down the centre. Cut out the shape required using a leaf or petal cutter.

**2** Dip the floral wire into edible glue (28-gauge is most commonly used, but on larger shapes you will require something a little more sturdy). Hold the leaf between your index finger and thumb. Insert the wire into the paste ridge. Vein using the appropriate veiner (see opposite).

**3** Soften the edge of the leaf/petal with a dogbone or ball tool (see Frilling and Softening, page 17). Give it some movement by twisting it a little.

### Linear leaves and petals

**1** Roll a piece of flowerpaste into a longish sausage. Dip a piece of wire into edible glue and pull it longways through the centre of the paste.

**2** Place the paste on a non-stick board and flatten it slightly with a palette knife. Roll the paste as thinly as possible either side of the wire, from the centre to the outside edges, using a piece of dowel or a mini rolling pin or Cel stick.

**3** Cut out the shape required, either freehand with scissors or with a cutter. Vein (see Veining, opposite) and soften the edges (see Frilling and Softening, page 17).

# Veining

There are several ways of veining petals and leaves using either a dresden tool, rubber veiners, a ceramic veining tool or a cardboard template and real leaf.

## Veining with a dresden tool

Place the leaf or petal on a petal pad. Using the thin end of the dresden tool and starting at the base, draw a line upwards to the outside edge of the leaf or petal.

## Using commercial veiners

**1** These are available in rubber and usually have two parts. To use one first follow steps 1–2 of Basic Leaves and Petals (opposite).

**2** Dust the veiner with cornflour (cornstarch) and place the shape on the bottom half of the mould. Press the top half of the mould down on the shape, squeezing it quite firmly to ensure a good vein.

**3** Continue with step 3 of Basic Leaves and Petals.

15

## Veining with a real leaf template

**1** Select the leaves or petals you require. Make sure they are undamaged, dry and clean. Attach them to a piece of thin card using double-sided tape so that the underside is uppermost.

**2** Leave the leaves or petals to dry out completely before cutting around the outside with a sharp pair of scissors – if you cut before the leaf has completely dried out it will shrink, leaving a sticky edge that sticks to the flowerpaste.

**3** Use the template to cut out your leaf shape by pressing gently into rolled out flowerpaste. Redefine the veins with a dresden tool.

## Veining with a ceramic veining/frilling tool

This tool has veins on its surface. Roll it over a leaf or petal to give a delicate texture. It's also good for frilling the edges of petals.

## MAKING HOMEMADE VEINERS

Making your own veiners from Silicone Plastique™ is great if you want to create lots of different leaves because it is much more cost-effective than buying veiners. Silicone Plastique™ is available from good sugarcraft suppliers and comes in two parts that are mixed together to create a rubbery substance that can be moulded. Homemade veiners are used in the same way as commercial ones.

**1** Mix the compound and the curing agent together in equal quantities and work together until blended. Only mix up enough for one or two leaves at a time. If you have to stop for any reason, put the mixed compound into a plastic bag and pop into the freezer. This will slow down the drying time. Roll it into roughly the shape of the leaf and then press a board covered in cling film against the shape to smooth the surface. Take care as the compound sticks to most surfaces.

**2** Press the underside of a real leaf against the compound, starting with the central vein. Make sure you don't get air trapped under the leaf. Trim off excess compound leaving a narrow margin around the edge. You can reuse the excess by rolling into a ball and starting again. Leave to dry completely. Remove the leaf from the mould and carefully wipe a thin layer of cold cream into the dry veiner.

**3** Mix up another batch of compound, slightly thicker this time.

**4** Roll out the compound to the same shape as before and smooth the surface. Starting at the central vein, press the compound into the veiner you have already made, being careful not to trap any air bubbles. Cut away excess and allow to dry.

**5** When this is completely set open the two halves, wipe away the cold cream and dust with cornflour (cornstarch).

## Cupping, frilling and softening

A dogbone or ball tool, or even a cocktail stick (toothpick), is used to define and soften petals and leaves.

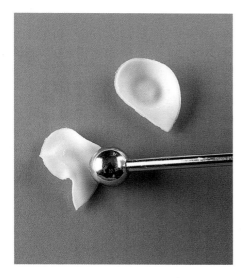

### Cupping

Place the petal on a petal pad and use the dogbone or ball tool to rub the centre of the petal in a circular movement to form a cup shape.

### Frilling and softening

The technique for frilling and softening is the same for both petals and leaves. Place the top side of the petal or leaf on a petal pad so the underside is uppermost. Take a dogbone or ball tool and run it back and forth on the outside edge only. This will soften the edge and lightly frill as well. If more frilling is required just apply a little more pressure. Working on the underside means that less definition of the top side is lost.

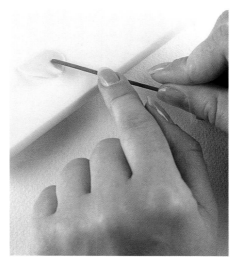

### Frilling and thinning down using a cocktail stock (toothpick)

Lightly dust your board with cornflour (cornstarch) and place your cut shape on the board near the edge. Round off one end of a cocktail stick with an emery board. Place the rounded end in the centre of the shape but on the edge, using this hand as your guide. Place the index finger of your other hand on top of the cocktail stick, and use this finger to roll the stick. This will start to frill the flowerpaste. Use the other hand to pick up the stick and move it along. You can also use a ceramic veining tool or needle tool for this.

## Glazing

Finished dry petals and leaves need to be glazed to give them a gentle sheen. It also prevents dusting powders from falling onto your finished cake. I use two different methods: steaming and using confectioner's glaze.

### Steaming

After the leaves or petals have been dusted with colour, gently pass them through the steam from a boiling kettle. This gives the paste a slight sheen and provides a good surface on which to glaze if you want more shine. Always allow your petals and leaves to dry completely after steaming before going onto the next process.

### Using confectioner's glaze

Confectioner's glaze is available from sugarcraft suppliers and can be used in various strengths. By mixing the glaze with high-strength alcohol, you can achieve different results. Full-strength glaze gives a high shine, most suited to berries and very shiny leaves. Three-quarter-strength glaze is made from one part alcohol to three parts glaze, giving a semi-gloss that's not too plasticky. Half-strength glaze is made from equal quantities of glaze and alcohol and gives a natural shine that is suited to most foliage and some buds. Quarter-strength glaze is three parts alcohol to one part glaze. This is used for less shiny leaves. It also takes away that flat, dusty appearance.

**1** Place confectioner's glaze and alcohol in a clean lidded jar, shake well. Leave to stand while the bubbles disperse.

**2** Dip the leaf or petal into the glaze, shake off the excess and leave to dry on kitchen towel. Alternatively, you can use a paintbrush, but you must steam the leaves or petals first and allow them to dry completely, otherwise you will get a streaky effect.

# freesia

Freesias are found in a variety of colours, from white, cream and yellow to mauve, pink and red. The colour of the stamens usually matches the petals. They have a wonderful, powerful scent.

## Materials

White, pale green and green flowerpaste

Dusting powders (petal dust) in the following colours: your choice for the flowers, bright green

22-, 26- and 28-gauge wires

Small white stamens

Edible glue

Light green florist's tape

## Equipment

Freesia cutter (AP Cutters F62)

Wire cutters

Fine scissors

Cocktail stick (toothpick) with one end rounded off

Dresden tool

Paintbrush

Small round-nosed pliers

Craft knife

## Stamens

**1** Take a tiny piece of white flowerpaste and attach to the ends of a stamen using a little edible glue. Roll each end into a tiny sausage shape and repeat to make another stamen. Cut in half so you have four stamens. Cut a piece of 26-gauge wire about 15 cm (6 in) long and attach the four stamens to one end using one-third-width tape. Leaving one stamen proud, carry on taping to form a little bump at the base of the stamens. Flatten the top of the longest stamen and cut it into three with a pair of fine scissors. Separate the stamens. Dust with the colour of your choice.

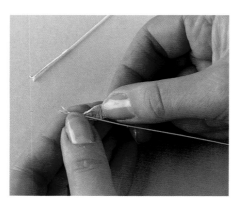

Attaching the stamens to the wire

## Petals

**2** Roll a piece of white flowerpaste quite thinly. Cut two shapes using the freesia cutter and cover one with a plastic bag. On a petal pad, separate the petals and then spread them out using the blunt end of a cocktail stick. Work down each side to thin down and widen. Leave the paste a little thicker in the middle. Cup the tops of the petals and vein down the centre of each petal using a dresden tool.

**3** Paint edible glue about a quarter of the way up each petal (from the base). Place the wired stamens on the petal shape. The bulb piece should be just below the line of the

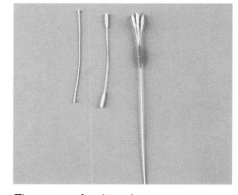

The stages of making the stamens

petals. Roll the petals around the bulb making sure they don't overlap. Hang upside down.

**4** Work the second shape in the same way. Take the petals and pull the bottom triangle carefully to widen the shape slightly. Brush with edible glue and wrap around the first petals, making sure they lie in between the first layer. Pinch to secure. Hang upside down until they are almost dry (this will allow them to open a little), then dust the flowers carefully with your chosen colour, leaving the bottom section white.

## Buds

**5** The buds vary in size and colour. The smaller ones are green and change colour as they get bigger. Cut several pieces of 28-gauge wire. Make tiny hooks at one end using round-nosed pliers. Roll a piece of pale green flowerpaste into a slender teardrop. Slightly point the top of the bulbous end. Make three cuts down the bud. Moisten the wire with edible glue, insert into the slender end of the bud and leave to dry.

**Note:** Make small buds using pale green flowerpaste. For bigger buds use cream flowerpaste and then dust these to match your flower colour.

## Calyx

**6** Shape a small piece of green flowerpaste (slightly darker than that used for the buds) into a cone. Open the wide end using the pointed end of a cocktail stick. Thin down the edges using the rounded end. Cut away two V shapes from the cone. Re-thin the edges. The calyx should now resemble a little beak. Paint a little edible glue inside the calyx. Push it up the wire and secure at the base of the flowers and buds.

## Assembly

**7** Start by taping two small buds one below the other. Carry on down the stem increasing the bud size as you go. Add the flowers. The buds and flowers should lie right and left as you look down the stem. If you want a long stem tape in a piece of 22-gauge wire as you put in your first flower. Bend the stem into a gentle curve. Dust the calyxes bright green. Steam and leave to dry.

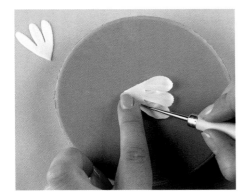

Veining with a dresden tool

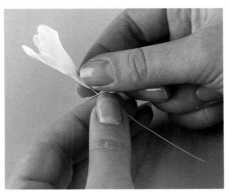

Wrapping the first shape around stamen

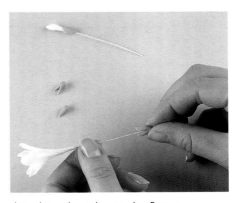

Attaching the calyx to the flower

# sunflower

These lovely flowers get their name from their habit of following the sun. In the morning they face east and during the day they track the sun until the evening when they face west. A field of bright sunflowers cannot fail to lift the spirits.

## Materials

Yellow, brown and green flowerpaste

Dusting powders (petal dust) in the following colours: lemon, brown, foliage green

22-, 24- and 30-gauge wire

Brown and light green florist's tape

Edible glue

Thick pipe cleaners

Kitchen towel torn into 5-mm (1/4-in) strips

## Equipment

Ruskus leaf cutter set (Fine Cut 5841)

Solomons seal veiner (SK Great Impressions)

Flower centre mould (Sugar City)

Rose petal cutters (Tinkertech 276-280)

Sunflower leaf cutter (Fine Cut 679)

Sunflower leaf veiner (Sugar City)

Wire cutters

Ball tool

Fine scissors

Tweezers

Paintbrush

## Petals

**1** Cut approximately 30 pieces of 30-gauge wire into 5-cm (2-in) lengths.

**2** Thinly roll out each piece of flowerpaste for the petals, leaving a ridge through the middle. Using the Ruskus leaf cutter, cut out each petal shape. Insert a 30-gauge wire moistened with edible glue, transfer to a petal pad and soften the edges using a ball tool. Vein using Solomons seal veiner and allow to dry with a slight curve. Dust with lemon dusting powder.

## Flower

**3** Take a piece of 22-gauge wire and bend one end into a ring, making sure the longer piece stays centrally within the ring.

**4** Cover a piece of 30-gauge wire with one-third-width brown florist's tape all the way along. Cut this into sections about 6 mm (1/4 in) long to make the stamens.

**5** Take a piece of brown flowerpaste about the size of a conker and form it into a domed shape. Press it into the largest flower centre mould. While it is still in there, moisten the ring of 22-gauge wire with a little edible glue and stick the stem into position. Carefully remove the whole centre from the mould. Cut little Vs around the edge of the flower centre.

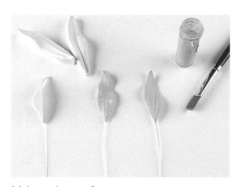
Making the sunflower petals

Cutting the wire to create stamens

Cutting V shapes into the flower centre

**6** Moisten one end of each stamen piece and use tweezers to place them in a double row around the edge of the centre.

**7** Dust the whole of the centre with brown. Moisten just the tips of the stamens with edible glue and dip these into lemon dusting powder. Pat off the excess and steam carefully. Leave to dry.

**8** Tape in a couple more 22-gauge wires and three pipe cleaners directly underneath the flower centre. Wrap torn kitchen towel around these to thicken the stem, then tape over this with full-width light green florist's tape.

**9** Take your petals and trim the wires. Moisten the end of the wire with edible glue and push the petals in one by one around the centre. Do two rows like this, making sure the petals of the second row are in between the petals of the first. Leave to dry. Steam again lightly.

## Calyx
**10** Thinly roll out a piece of green flowerpaste. Cut out several shapes using the smallest rose petal cutter. Transfer one shape at a time to a petal pad, keeping the others

covered. Soften the edge very gently without frilling it; indent the rounded end slightly. Using a little edible glue stick the shape into place so the pointed end is about one-third of the way up the petals. Continue all the way around. Do a second and third row in the same way. You should now be down around the stem of the flower. Leave to dry.

Dust the back of the flower using foliage green and steam.

## Leaves
**11** These large leaves need a 24-gauge wire. Using the sunflower leaf cutter and veiner, make the leaves. When these are finished tape two or three to the stem of the flower. Dust with foliage green.

Inserting the stamens

Attaching the petals

Adding the calyx

21

# carnation

The spray carnation is part of the *dianthus* family and is a small, multi-headed version of the standard carnation. It comes in a wide range of colours and is used a lot in flower arranging as it keeps well after being cut.

## Materials

Your choice of flowerpaste colour for the flowers, plus green

Dusting powders (petal dust) in the following colours: your choice for the flowers, foliage green, eucalyptus

26-gauge wire

Light green florist's tape

Edible glue

## Equipment

Blossom cutter (Tinkertech 521)

Wire cutters

Small round-nosed pliers

Craft knife

Cocktail stick (toothpick) with one end rounded off

Paintbrush

Fine scissors

Dresden tool

## Flower

**1** Take a piece of wire approximately 15 cm (6 in) long and make a small hook at one end using round-nosed pliers. Wrap a piece of one-third-width florist's tape round the hook several times until it looks like a match.

**2** Roll out a piece of flowerpaste in your chosen flower colour. Cut out three shapes using the blossom cutter and set two aside, covered with a plastic bag. With a craft knife, make a series of cuts into the paste extending the indentations around the edges. Using the blunt end of a cocktail stick, frill the outside edges. Push the wire through the centre of the shape. Brush edible glue over half of the shape and take the shape to nearly the top of the wire. Fold it in half upwards, then fold half of the half into the centre and secure with edible glue. Turn the shape around and repeat with the remaining quarter.

**3** Cut and frill the second shape as before. Push this carefully up the

wire and secure underneath the first layer with a little edible glue. Repeat with the third shape. Leave to dry.

## Calyx

**4** Shape a piece of green flowerpaste into a cone. Using a cocktail stick, hollow out the pointed end of the cone. Make sure you get the edges very fine. Cut five triangles from the thin edge of the paste using a pair of fine pointed scissors. Thin the points using a cocktail stick. Brush the inside of the calyx with edible glue and thread it onto the wire to meet the flower. Make two tiny cuts at the base of the calyx on opposite sides using the scissors.

**5** Dust either the whole flower or just the top edges to give two contrasting colours. Carefully dust the calyx with foliage green. Steam and leave to dry.

## Leaves

**6** Carnations have tiny pairs of spear-like leaves down their stems. If you are using carnations in an arrangement, you may not need to

Frilling the petals with a cocktail stick

Folding the shape in half upwards

Adding the next layer

Dusting the calyx

include the leaves but if you want to make them, make several pairs of small linear leaves (see page 14).

**7** Using a dresden tool, mark a central vein down each leaf. Bend slightly and leave to dry. Take the flower and, using one-third-width tape, start to tape a little way down the stem. Tape in one pair of leaves then, immediately underneath the leaves, make a little bump. Tape a little further and then add another pair of leaves. Repeat the taping process so you have a small bump under each pair of leaves. Very carefully dust the leaves and stem with foliage green and a little eucalyptus over the top. Steam and allow to dry.

# open rose

Open roses are lovely flowers. In England the Tudor rose is probably the most famous, but roses go back a very long way – fossilized remains show that they pre-date mankind!

## Materials

Pale green and pale yellow flowerpaste

Dusting powders (petal dust) in the following colours: spring green, lemon, red, foliage green

22- 24- and 28-gauge wire

Edible glue

Seedhead stamens

Hi-tack non-toxic glue

Light green florist's tape

One-third strength glaze

## Equipment

Rose petal cutters (Tinkertech Golden Wings 771–775)

Rose petal cutters (Tinkertech 276-280)

Rose petal veiners (SK Great Impressions)

Rose calyx cutters (Tinkertech 246, 245)

Rose leaf cutters (Jem green set)

Rose leaf veiners (SK Great Impressions Large Tea Rose)

Tweezers

Ball tool

Fine scissors

Small round-nosed pliers

Cone tool

## Centre and stamens

**1** Shape a small piece of pale green flowerpaste into a cone. Moisten the end of a 22-gauge wire, and push this into the bulbous end of the cone. Lightly texture the surface of the cone with tweezers. Leave to dry then dust with spring green.

**2** Divide the stamens into small groups, levelling the heads. Apply glue to the middle section of the stamens. Spread this up both ends of the threads leaving about 1 cm (1/2 in) clear at each end. Let this dry a little and cut in half. Trim to just below the glue line. Allow to dry.

**3** Apply a little drop of glue to each stamen group and arrange around the green centre. Squeeze the stamens against the wire to secure. Leave to dry. Bend the stamens inwards using a pair of tweezers.

**4** Dust the tips of the stamens with lemon and the threads with red.

## Petals

**5** Thinly roll out a piece of pale yellow flowerpaste, leaving a ridge through the centre. Cut out the petal shape using the rose petal cutter and insert a 28-gauge wire moistened with edible glue. Vein using the rose petal veiner. Transfer the petal to a petal pad. Cup down each side of the central vein using a ball tool, then soften the edges.

Texturing the surface of the centre

Attaching the stamens

**6** Make four more petals in the same way and leave them to firm up a little. Dust the petals, working from the base upwards, with a little lemon. Add a touch of spring green close to the wire.

**7** Using half-width florist's tape, tape the petals around the stamens. They should be slightly flexible still, so they can be reshaped if necessary. Leave to dry.

## Calyx

**8** Take a piece of pale green flowerpaste and form into a Mexican hat. Roll the paste from the centre outwards to make it finer.

**9** Cut out the calyx using the larger calyx cutter. Place on the petal pad and elongate each section using the ball tool. Cup the centre of each sepal. Cut fine lines into the edges of four of the sepals. Dust outside the calyx sepals with foliage green.

**10** Make a hole in the centre of the calyx using a cone tool. Moisten the centre with edible glue and thread it up the wire. Secure behind the rose petals with the sepals in between the gaps of the petals. Bend the tips back slightly. Dust the rest of the calyx with foliage green.

## Buds

**11** Make a small hook in the end of a piece of 24-gauge wire using round-nosed pliers. Form a small piece of pale yellow flowerpaste into a cone. Moisten the hooked end of the wire and insert into the thick end of the cone. Leave to dry.

**12** Thinly roll out a piece of pale yellow flowerpaste and cut three rose petal shapes. Vein and soften the edges with a ball tool. Moisten the first petal with edible glue and wrap it around the cone tightly, leaving the petal proud at the top and the edge slightly open. Moisten the bottom of the next petal. Tuck it into the open edge of the petal before and wrap it halfway around. Take the next petal. Moisten the bottom. Tuck in and wrap both petals around. Curl this final petal back a little. Leave to dry.

**13** Dust the bud with lemon. It should be a little darker than the flower. Add the calyx as for the flower (using a smaller calyx cutter).

**14** Using green flowerpaste and the rose leaf cutters and veiners, make the leaves. When dry, dust with foliage green.

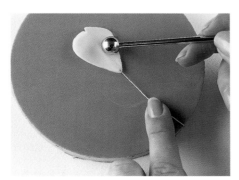

Cupping the petal with a ball tool

Assembling the rose

Making the calyx

# rose

The beautiful rose, shown here as a full-blown flower, is associated with romantic love and desire. This red rose would look perfect on a Valentine's Day celebration cake.

## Materials

Pale pink and green flowerpaste

Dusting powders (petal dust) in the following colours: aubergine, foliage green

22-, 26- and 28-gauge wire

Edible glue

Light green florist's tape

One-third strength confectioner's glaze

## Equipment

Rose petal cutters (Tinkertech 549-551)

Rose petal veiners (SK Great Impressions)

Rose calyx cutters (Tinkertech 246, 245)

Rose leaf cutters (Jem black set)

Rose leaf veiners (SK Great Impressions)

Wire cutters

Small round-nosed pliers

Ball tool

Paintbrush

## Colouring Note

Use flowerpaste that is a shade paler than you require for the finished rose, then when the flower is dry, you can dust it with a stronger colour.

## Flower centre

**1** Form a piece of flowerpaste into a cone. Make a hook in the end of a half-length piece of 22-gauge wire using round-nosed pliers. Moisten the hook with edible glue and insert into the broad end of the cone. Allow to dry. For the flower the cone should be no longer than the smallest petal, and for the buds about 5 mm ($^{1}/_{4}$ in) shorter.

## Petals

**2** To make the first layer of petals, roll a piece of flowerpaste quite thinly. Cut out four petals using the smallest of the rose petal cutters. Place one petal on a petal pad and cover the others with a plastic bag to keep them soft. Soften the edges using a ball tool and vein with the rose petal veiner. Place in the plastic bag. Repeat the process for the other petals.

**3** Moisten the first petal with edible glue and wrap it tightly around the cone, making sure the cone is covered and that the tip is not visible. If you are making a bud, roll back the edge of the petal slightly.

Inserting a wire into the cone

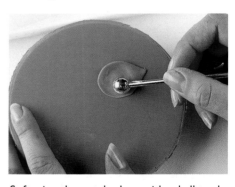
Softening the petal edges with a ball tool

Wrapping the first petal round the cone

**4** To make the second layer, take the remaining petals and use a paintbrush to moisten each one with edible glue down its left-hand side, about one-third to half the length from the tip. Place the rose cone onto the centre of the petal. Secure the moistened edge and wrap the petal around approximately one-third of the cone. Tuck in the next petal. Tuck the final petal in under the previous petal and wrap it around – it should go over the first petal. Secure with a little edible glue. Try to keep the petals fairly tight and make sure the final layer is slightly higher than the first. Roll back the edges of the petals a little. If you are using this size for a bud, bring one petal out slightly further than the other two.

**5** Repeat steps 2-4 to make the third layer of petals.

**6** Make the fourth layer in the same way but using the next size cutter. This stage can also be used for a larger bud – if so the petals need not be as tight and the edges of the petals can come back a little further.

**7** You are now at the half rose stage. Cut out three more petals using the largest cutter. Cup the centre of each one using the ball

tool. The petals go over the joins of the previous layer and the edges can come back much further this time.

**8** To make the rose full blown you need to wire the last petals. Cut five half-length pieces of 26-gauge wire. Roll a piece of flowerpaste reasonably thinly leaving a ridge through the centre. Cut out the rose petal shape using the largest cutter. Moisten the end of a wire with edible glue and insert it into the ridge. Vein using a rose petal veiner. Soften the edges with a ball tool and cup the centre. Curl the edges of the petals

back. Repeat with the remaining four petals and leave for a while so they firm up. Tape these in underneath the other petals with full-width florist's tape. Leave to dry.

**9** Colour the rose with aubergine dusting powder.

## Calyx
**10** Make and secure the calyx following steps 8-10 of Open Rose (see page 25). Steam and let dry.

## Leaves
**11** Use the rose leaf cutters and veiners to make the leaves from green flowerpaste. Use 28-gauge wire. Dust the leaves with foliage green dusting powder, steam and leave to dry.

**12** Tape the leaves to the flower stem and glaze the petals and leaves with one-third strength confectioner's glaze.

Adding petal layers to the cone

Taping in the wired petals

27

# iris

This is the smallest member of the iris family, appearing in early spring. It is a very dainty plant and can be found in deep purple or pale blue and yellow. It also has very interesting square leaves.

## Materials

White, yellow, mauve and green
  flowerpaste
Dusting powders (petal dust) in the
  following colours: purple, foliage
  green, black
24-, 26- and 30-gauge wires
Dark green florist's tape
Edible glue
Clear alcohol (gin or vodka)
One-third-strength confectioner's glaze

## Equipment

Iris cutters (Fine Cut set 358)
Wire cutters
Ball tool
Cocktail stick (toothpick) with one end
  rounded off
Dresden tool
Needle tool (optional)
Very fine paintbrush
Two Cel sticks

## Flower

**1** Cut six 13-cm (5-in) lengths of 30-gauge wire. Thinly roll a piece of white flowerpaste, leaving a ridge through the middle. Using the narrowest iris cutter, cut three petal shapes. Insert a wire moistened with edible glue into the ridge of the petal. Place the petal on your board and soften the edges using a ball tool. Use a cocktail stick to thin down the edges even more. Be careful not to lose the shape of the petal.

**2** Place the petal on a petal pad and, using the sharp end of a dresden tool, indent a central vein lengthways. Leave to dry, curving slightly inwards.

**3** To make the lower section of the flower, follow the instructions as above, using the spoon-shaped cutter. Use a cocktail stick to fan out the rounded ends only – do not touch the edges. Place the petal on the petal pad and indent the central vein hard so the sides come up to form a channel. Curve the shape down-wards and leave to dry completely.

Widening the petals with a cocktail stick

**4** Roll out another piece of flowerpaste, this time leaving out the ridge. Cut out the last shape (a long thin heart), thin down and frill the two lobes only. Cup the two lobes to make them curl upwards. Turn the shape over. Using the dresden tool, vein the centre line hard lengthways. Take the dry bottom petal, paint the upper edges with edible glue and place the new petal on top, edges joining. This will form a hollow tube. Leave to dry.

**5** Dust all the petals with purple dusting powder. Take a tiny piece of yellow flowerpaste and roll into a cigar shape. Using a needle tool or cocktail stick press the pointed end down and along to make a division lengthways. Stick this to the lower petal just inside the opening using edible glue.

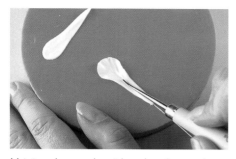

Veining the petals with a dresden tool

Placing the top petal on the bottom one

Placing yellow flowerpaste in the lip

Assembling the flower

Attaching the bottom of the flower

**6** To create the white dashes on the petals put a little clear alcohol into a dish. Dip a paintbrush in, wipe clean and dab onto the petals, lifting away the purple colour.

## Assembly

**7** Using one-third-width florist's tape, tape the three upright petals together, making sure they curve inwards. Next, tape the three lower ones in between the gaps. Now tape in three 20-cm (8-in) lengths of 24-gauge wire immediately under the petals to lengthen the stem.

**8** Roll a very small piece of mauve flowerpaste into a teardrop. Hollow out a little with a cocktail stick. Thread up the wires. Brush inside of cone with a little edible glue. Gently mould this into the back of the petals, and dust to match the flower.

**9** Roll out a piece of pale green flowerpaste and cut out three narrow spear shapes. Soften the edges with a ball tool. Moisten the stem of the flower with a little edible glue and attach the spear shapes down the stem.

## Leaves

**10** Roll green flowerpaste into a long, thick sausage. Moisten the 26-gauge wire with edible glue and thread into the sausage shape. Roll on your board to make it thinner. Place two small Cel sticks either side of the flowerpaste shape and squeeze. Turn the flowerpaste and repeat the process. You should now have a square shape. Leave to dry and then dust with foliage green mixed with a little black. Lightly steam all the flowers and leaves and leave to dry. Glaze with one-third-strength confectioner's glaze and arrange as required.

29

# viola

These flowers are related to the sweet violet. They can be found in a range of colours from white, cream and yellow, to purple and blue, and in combinations of the above. They are also edible. Pansies are made in the same way, only using a larger cutter.

## Materials

White and green flowerpaste

Dusting powder (petal dust) in the following colours: baby maize, mimosa, lavender, African violet, rainforest

26-gauge wire

Edible glue

Light green florist's tape

Small yellow stamens

One-third-strength confectioner's glaze

## Equipment

Six-petal flower cutter (Orchard Products N2)

Calyx cutter (Tinkertech 304 and 406)

Rose petal cutter (Tinkertech 276-280)

Leaf cutter (Orchard Products OL1-OL4)

Rose leaf veiners (SK Great Impressions)

Cocktail stick (toothpick) with one end rounded off

Dresden tool

Wire cutters

Small round-nosed pliers

Tweezers

Ball tool

Making the flower (Mexican hat method)

Curving the bottom petal

Pulling the wire through the flower

## Flower

**1** Form a Mexican hat shape from a piece of white flowerpaste. Cut out one shape using the six-petal flower cutter. Dampen the edge of one of the petals with edible glue and stick this to the one next to it. Using the blunt end of a cocktail stick, broaden the shape to make a nest. Repeat with the other petals.

**2** Make a small hole in the centre using a dresden tool and then curve the sides of the bottom petal gently.

**3** Roll the back of the flower into a slender cone. Take a piece of 26-gauge wire about 8 cm (3 in) long. Tape this with one-third-width light green florist's tape. Make a small hook at the end using round-nosed pliers. Moisten the hook with a little edible glue and pull through the flower centre diagonally.

**4** Stick a small stamen into the throat of the flower using tweezers. Leave to dry. Bend the wire from the back flower to make a crook. Dust with either baby maize and mimosa or lavender and African violet.

## Calyx

**5** Roll a small piece of green flowerpaste thinly, and cut one shape using the larger of the two calyx cutters. Place on a petal pad and slightly lengthen each lobe using a ball tool. Allow to dry.

**6** Dust the calyx with rainforest. Moisten the back of the flower with edible glue and slide the calyx up the wire and attach to the flower.

**7** Cut a second shape using the smaller cutter. Place on the petal pad. Slightly lengthen each lobe using the ball tool and then dust with rainforest. Moisten the back of the first calyx with edible glue and slide the second one up the wire and secure with the lobes pointing upwards. Steam and leave to dry and then glaze with one-third-strength confectioner's glaze.

## Bud

**8** Roll a very small piece of white flowerpaste into a cigar shape. Attach to a piece of 26-gauge wire.

Leave to dry. Roll out a piece of white flowerpaste. Cut out a shape using a small rose petal cutter. Thin down and wrap around the cigar. Leave to dry. Dust with the colour of your choice. Make a calyx but this time only use the smallest calyx cutter and elongate the first one slightly more than the second.

**9** Using the leaf cutter and veiners, make leaves. Dust with rainforest, steam and leave to dry. Glaze using one-third-strength confectioner's glaze. Secure the leaves to the stem. Start with the smaller ones at the top and work down, taping them in pairs or sets of three.

Inserting the stamen into the flower

Sliding the calyx up the wire

Dusting the flower

# primrose

This pretty pale yellow flower, usually with an orange centre, appears early in the season. It tells you that spring is on the way. It is very simple to make and can be used on its own or with its leaves, although they work best in small clusters.

## Materials

Yellow and green flowerpaste

Dusting powders (petal dust) in the following colours: baby maize, lemon yellow, burgundy, foliage green

26-gauge wire

Cornflour (cornstarch)

Small white stamens dusted with spring green

Edible glue

Light green florist's tape

## Equipment

Primrose flower cutter (Tinkertech 152)

Primrose leaf cutter (Fine Cut 529, 530, 535, 540)

Primrose leaf veiners (SK Great Impressions)

Small Cel stick

Cone tool

Cocktail stick (toothpick) with one end rounded off

Ball tool

Paintbrush

Small pointed scissors

Tweezers

## Flower

**1** Shape a piece of yellow flowerpaste into a Mexican hat. Make sure the point remains quite slender. Place onto a board and using a small Cel stick roll the paste thinly from the point outwards. Cut out the flower shape, using a primrose flower cutter, making sure the point is in the centre of the cutter.

**2** Make a hole in the centre of the flower using a cone tool. Dust your index finger with a little cornflour. Place one of the petals on here. Take a cocktail stick and with the point towards the centre roll one side of the petal, then the other. Repeat on all the petals. Cup slightly using a ball tool.

**3** Take a piece of 26-gauge wire approximately 10 cm (4 in) long. Dip into edible glue and pull through the centre of the flower. Insert a stamen into the centre. Leave to dry. Dust with baby maize, and dust the centre of the flower with the lemon yellow.

## Calyx

**4** Roll a small piece of green flowerpaste into a teardrop shape.

Making the flower (Mexican hat method)

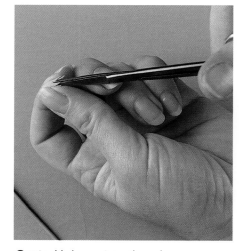

Cutting V shapes into the calyx

Using the sharp end of a cocktail stick, open up the pointed end of the paste. Roll it on your index finger to hollow out the cone. Use scissors to cut five V shapes from the cone and roll each one to thin.

**5** Brush the inside of the calyx with a little edible glue; push it up the wire. Secure just below the top of the flower. Using tweezers, pinch a line up the middle of the points the full length of the calyx. Steam and leave to dry.

**6** Tape the stem with one-third-width light green tape, gently dust with burgundy dusting powder (primroses have one or the other coloured stem).

## Leaves

**7** Make leaves using the primrose leaf cutters and veiners. Dust with foliage green, steam and let dry.

Using tweezers to pinch lines in the calyx

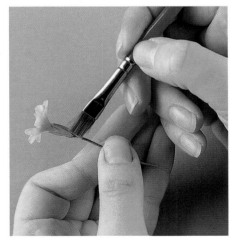

Dusting the calyx with burgundy powder

# daffodil

The daffodil is sometimes referred to as the Lent lily as it arrives in early spring. There are many varieties of daffodil with different colour combinations so once you have mastered this flower, try experimenting with other varieties.

## Materials

Yellow and green flowerpaste

Dusting powders (petal dust) in the following colours: primrose, lemon, spring green, autumn gold, nutkin brown, foliage green, eucalyptus

24- and 26-gauge wire

Small stamens

Light green and white florist's tape

Yellow Sugartex

Edible glue

## Equipment

Bridal lily cutter (FMM 2)

Daffodil petal veiner (SK Great Impressions)

Lily leaf veiner (SK Great Impressions)

Wire cutters

Cel stick

Cone tool

Ball tool

Cocktail stick (toothpick) with one end rounded off

Paintbrush

Icing tube/tip

Craft knife

Attaching the stamens to wire

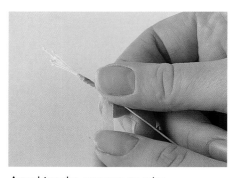
Making the petals (Mexican hat method)

Frilling the daffodil trumpet

## Flower

**1** Take a piece of 24-gauge wire approximately 25 cm (10 in) long. Secure six stamens to the end using one-third-width light green tape. Leave one slightly higher than the others. Brush these with edible glue and dip into yellow Sugartex.

**2** Shape a piece of yellow flowerpaste into a Mexican hat, making sure the point is fairly slender. Place on your board and using a small Cel stick, roll the paste from the point outwards. Using the bridal lily flower cutter, cut one shape. Make a fairly wide hole in the centre of the flower using a cone tool. On a petal pad use a ball tool to elongate the petals. Place the flower back on the board. Use a cocktail stick to broaden each petal. Vein with the petal veiner and soften the edges with the ball tool. Bring three alternate petals inwards. Brush a little edible glue at the bottom of the stamens and pull these through the centre of the flower. Indent a small ring around the bottom of the flower about 5 mm (1/4 in) up from the base.

centre of the flower and drop the trumpet into the hole. Secure and leave to dry.

**4** Cut two pieces of 24-gauge wire and tape to the base to thicken the stem. Tape the whole stem.

**5** Dust the flower petals with primrose dusting powder. Dust the trumpet with lemon and the back slender piece with spring green. Steam and leave to dry.

**6** Make the sheath by cutting a piece of white florist's tape about 5 cm (2 in) long. Dust with autumn gold dusting powder. Cut one end into a spear shape and twist. Dust the tip with nutkin brown. Paint very feint lines down the sheath using the same colour. Attach to the back of the flower and bend the head of flower down slightly.

## Buds

**7** Tape together three pieces of 26-gauge wire. Make a slender cone using yellow flowerpaste. Taper off one end to a more pointed shape. Make three cuts lengthways using a craft knife. Moisten the end of the wire and insert it into the narrower end. Leave to dry. Dust with primrose powder and a little spring green. Make and attach sheath as for the flower. Bend wire at a slight angle, so the bud faces upwards. Steam and leave to dry.

## Leaves

**8** Make linear leaves (see page 14). Dust with foliage green with a little eucalyptus over the top. Use a lily leaf veiner for the veins. Steam and allow to dry.

**3** Roll another piece of yellow flowerpaste quite thinly. Cut a trumpet shape using the template on page 78. Vein and frill the

outside edge using a cocktail stick. Brush edible glue down one side and wrap around an icing tube/tip and join the two edges. Moisten the

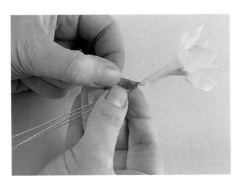

Taping in extra wires to the stem

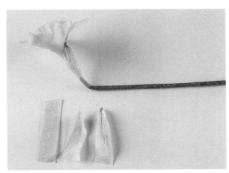

Making the sheath

# daisy

The daisy's original name was 'Day's eye' as it opens in the morning when the sun comes up and then closes in the evening when the sun goes down again. It is a simple little flower and very easy to make.

## Materials

Green, white and yellow flowerpaste

Dusting powders (petal dust) in the following colours: foliage green, pink, spring green, rainforest, burgundy

28-gauge wire

Light green florist's tape

Edible glue

Yellow pollen powder

## Equipment

Calyx cutter (Tinkertech 406)

Daisy cutter (Tinkertech 106)

Wire cutters

Small round-nosed pliers

Ball tool

Paintbrush

Craft knife

Cocktail stick (toothpick) with one end rounded off

## Calyx

**1** Cut a piece of 28-gauge wire about 8 cm (3 in) long. Make a tiny hook at one end using the round-nosed pliers.

**2** Shape a small piece of green flowerpaste into a Mexican hat. Keep it short and not too pointed. Cut out the calyx using the calyx cutter. Place on a petal pad and soften each point with a ball tool. Moisten the hooked end of the wire with edible glue and pull down through the middle of the calyx. Make a slight hollow in the middle with the ball tool. Leave to dry.

**3** Thicken the stem by covering it with one-third-width light green tape. Dust the back of the calyx with foliage green.

## Flower

**4** Roll a piece of white flowerpaste very finely. Cut one daisy shape using the daisy cutter. Divide each petal into two lengthways using a craft knife. Take a cocktail stick and thin down each petal until nearly transparent. Transfer the shape to the petal pad. Take your ball tool and using the small end stroke each petal from the tip inwards to make them curve. Paint

Making a hook at one end of the wire

Thinning down the petals

a little edible glue onto the calyx and stick daisy shape into place.

**5** Repeat step 4 and attach this second flower to layer one, making sure the petals of the second layer lie in between the petals of the first layer. Leave to dry.

**6** To make the centre, take a small piece of yellow flowerpaste and roll it into a ball. Flatten it slightly and attach to the middle of the flower with edible glue. With a cocktail stick prick the surface of the centre. Paint a little edible glue on to the centre and sprinkle with yellow pollen dust. Tap away excess.

**7** Dust the tips of the daisy petals with pink, and add a touch of spring green to the petals where they meet the yellow centre. Steam and let dry.

## Leaves
**8** Using the templates provided on page 78, make the leaves and let dry. Dust with rainforest and just catch the edges with burgundy. Steam and leave to dry.

Attaching the centre of the flower

Dusting the tips of the petals

# holly & ivy

Holly and ivy were believed to have magical powers long before they became associated with Christmas. Not all holly has red berries – sometimes they are yellow. There are two varieties of ivy used here – they have different shaped leaves. The trailing ivy uses the cutters and the ivy with the berries uses a template (see page 78).

## Materials

Green and red flowerpaste

Dusting powders (petal dust) in the following colours: foliage green, black, aubergine

20-, 26- and 30-gauge wires

Light green and beige florist's tape

Full- and half-strength confectioner's glaze

Edible glue

## Equipment

Baby ivy leaf cutters (Jem)

Ivy leaf veiners succinata (SK Great Impressions)

Holly leaf cutters (AP Cutters)

Needle tool or round-headed pin

Wire cutters

Paintbrush

Tweezers

Small round-nosed pliers

## Ivy

**1** Cut out the ivy leaves using the ivy cutters or the template provided. Dust the leaves with a mix of foliage green and a little black dusting powder, then vein with the ivy veiner or a needle tool. Dust a little aubergine around the edges. Steam and leave to dry. Glaze using half-strength confectioner's glaze.

**2** Tape the wire underneath each leaf using half-width green tape approximately 2.5 cm (1 in). Starting with one small leaf, tape onto a piece of 26-gauge wire using one-third-width beige tape. Carry on down the stem. The leaf size should vary on each stem. Mostly the leaves are single but occasionally they will be in pairs. Dust a little aubergine onto the stem where the leaves join in. Steam and let dry.

## Ivy berries

**3** Cut several short lengths of 30-gauge wire. Roll a small piece of green flowerpaste into a ball. Insert a piece of wire moistened with edible glue through the ball so that it almost comes out at the top to make a point. Using a pair of tweezers pinch in fine lines at the top to make a pentagon shape.

**4** Tape the wire underneath each

Scratching out the veins

Taping leaves onto a stem

Pinching out the top of the berries

wire and make tiny hooks at one end using round-nosed pliers. Roll small balls of red flowerpaste. Brush the hooked end of the wire with edible glue and pull it through the berry so it is just below the surface. Leave to dry.

**8** Using a little black colouring, paint the indent where the wire went through at the top. Dip into full-strength glaze. Leave to dry.

**9** Berries can be in large clusters or just one or two here and there, so it is up to you to decide on quantity. Tape the wire underneath each leaf and berry, a little way down using one-third-width light green florist's tape. Take two leaves. Tape them one just above the other, then carry on down adding leaves and berries as you go. If a larger spray is needed add in another small stem.

## Variations
Both holly and ivy have variegated forms. To make variegated leaves, use cream flowerpaste and either paint or dust on the green colour when they are dry. Steam and varnish as before.

berry using half-width green tape. Dust the berries with a mix of green and aubergine and a little black on top. Tape the berries together in bunches. Steam and leave to dry.

**5** Using one-third-width beige tape, tape a bunch of berries to a piece of 20-gauge wire. Add in leaves and more berries. Dust the stem with green powder and steam as before.

## Holly
**6** Using the holly cutters, make the leaves. Soften the leaf edges and pinch the points to redefine. Use the same powder mix used for the ivy to dust the holly leaves. Steam and leave to dry. Glaze using half-strength glaze.

## Holly berries
**7** Cut short lengths of 30-gauge

Taping berries together

Glazing the holly leaves

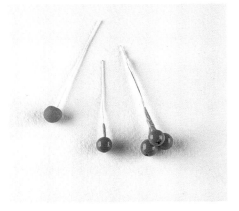

Making the holly berries

# christmas rose

Despite its name, the Christmas rose doesn't usually appear until January. They come in white, shades of pink and green. Some varieties also have spots.

## Materials

Pale green and white flowerpaste

Dusting powders (petal dust) in the following colours: mimosa, spring green, cyclamen, leaf, black, foliage green

26-, 28- and 30-gauge wire

Small seedhead stamens

Light green florist's tape

Hi-tack non-toxic glue

Edible glue

One-third strength confectioner's glaze

## Equipment

Daisy cutter (Tinkertech 106)

Christmas rose petal cutter (Fine Cut 546)

Christmas rose petal veiner (SK Great Impressions)

Virginia creeper leaf cutters (Kit Box)

Clematis Montana leaf veiner (SK Great Impressions)

Wire cutters

Scissors

Cocktail stick (toothpick) with one end rounded off

Paintbrush

Tweezers

Ball tool

## Pistil

**1** Cut a piece of 26-gauge wire about 13 cm (5 in) long. Cut five tiny points from a piece of florist's tape and attach this to the wire.

**2** Take around 25 stamens and glue together using hi-tack glue, leaving about 1 cm (1/2 in) clear at each end. Trim to just below the glue line. While still damp wrap around the pistil. Secure with a piece of half-width florist's tape. Dust the stamen tops with mimosa.

## Calyx

**3** Roll out a piece of pale green flowerpaste quite thinly. Cut out one shape using the daisy cutter. Broaden each section with a cocktail stick. Brush a tiny drop of edible glue into the centre of each section and pinch the edges in with tweezers. Bring this shape up behind the stamens and secure.

## Petals

**4** Cut five pieces of 30-gauge wire about 15 cm (6 in) long. Roll out a piece of white flowerpaste quite thinly, leaving a ridge through the centre. Cut out a petal using the Christmas rose petal cutter. Insert a piece of wire moistened with edible glue. Vein using the Christmas rose petal veiner. Transfer to a petal pad and soften the edges using a ball tool. Leave to dry with the petal curving gently forwards. Repeat for the remaining four petals.

**5** Dust the centre of each petal with spring green and just touch the base with cyclamen. To tape the petals around the centre, put the first one in, leave a gap and tape in the second one. Tape the next two beside this one, and the last one in the gap that is left.

Making the pistil from florist's tape

## Sepals

**6** Make two of these, following the instructions for the petals, but, using a pair of scissors, cut them into a spear shape. They should be quite small. Dust with leaf and cyclamen and tape behind the petals.

**7** Tape down the stem a couple of times using half-width tape to thicken. Dust the stem with cyclamen. Steam and leave to dry.

## Leaves

**8** Using the Virginia creeper cutters and clematis leaf veiner, make the leaves from green flowerpaste. Dust the leaves with black mixed with foliage green and then tape together in sets of three or five. Dust the stem and bottom of leaves with cyclamen. Steam, leave to dry and varnish with one-third strength confectioner's glaze.

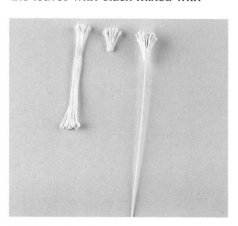

Attaching the stamens

Pinching the calyx into shape

Making the Christmas rose petals

# lily

Lilies are a large group of flowers with a vast colour range, from pure white to yellow and vivid oranges, reds and pinks. Use flowerpaste in a paler shade than you want the finished flower to be. Here the steps are for a classic pink lily while the finished shot shows a brilliant orange flower.

## Materials

Your choice of flowerpaste colours for the flowers, plus green and brown

Dusting powders (petal dust) in the following colours: brown, your choice for the petals, spring green, burgundy, foliage green

22-, 28- and 30-gauge wires

Edible glue

Light green florist's tape

Clear alcohol (gin or vodka)

Gum glue

One-third-strength confectioner's glaze

## Equipment

Lily cutters (Fine Cut 372)

Lily petal veiners (SK Great Impressions)

Lily leaf cutters (Fine Cut 371-373)

Wire cutters

Craft knife

Paintbrush

Ball tool

Tweezers

## Pistil

**1** Cut a piece of 26-gauge wire to about 15 cm (6 in) long. Take a piece of pale green flowerpaste and roll it into a 10-cm (4-in) sausage, then shape a bulbous end and a pointed end. Dip the wire into edible glue and pull it lengthways through the centre of the paste. Taper the paste at the top end, making sure it remains smooth. Take another small piece of light green flowerpaste. Roll it into a ball and squash to make it a little flatter. With a craft knife make three even cuts towards the centre to create a trefoil. Attach to the top of the pistil and dust carefully with brown. The complete pistil should be around two-thirds the length of the petals.

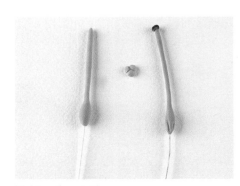

Making the pistil

## Stamens

**2** Cut six pieces of 30-gauge wire to 7.5 cm (3 in) long. Bend 5 mm (1/4 in) of the wire at a right angle. Then bend the short piece back on itself to make a T shape.

**3** Roll a tiny piece of brown flowerpaste into a sausage and taper both ends. Make a small cut lengthways into the sausage. Brush the T shape with a little edible glue and attach the sausage. Leave to dry, then brush with edible glue and dip into brown dusting powder. Tap off excess. Lightly steam and leave to dry. Repeat to make six stamens. Arrange the stamens around the pistil at equal intervals and tape using light green florist's tape.

Making the stamens

## Petals

**4** Cut six pieces of 26-gauge wire about 13 cm (5 in) long. Roll out a piece of flowerpaste in your chosen colour. Leave a ridge through the centre lengthways. Cut out the petal shapes, you need three of each size. Insert a wire moistened with edible glue halfway in each petal, vein and transfer to a petal pad. Using a ball tool, soften the edges. Leave to dry, curving slightly backwards.

**5** Dust the petals with the colour of your choice. Dust the base of the petals with spring green. Some lilies have burgundy dots on them. You can do this by mixing burgundy powder with clear alcohol and painting on once everything is dry.

**6** Tape the three widest petals under the stamens and the others in the three gaps remaining. Steam and leave to dry.

## Leaves

**7** Make linear leaves using the lily leaf cutters (see page 14). Dust with foliage green and steam.

## Buds

**8** Take a piece of 22-gauge wire approximately 15 cm (6 in) long. Make a hook at one end. Mould a piece of green flowerpaste into a bud shape. Pinch lengthways on three sides to make a more triangular shape. Take a pair of tweezers and pinch 1 cm ($^1/_2$ in) lengthways between the divisions. Moisten the wire with edible glue and insert into the bud. Dust with spring green. Steam and leave to dry. Varnish with one-third-strength glaze. Tape the stem using half-width tape.

## Assembly

**9** To assemble, start with a bud at the top, add a couple of small leaves, then your flower and more leaves.

Attaching stamens to the pistil

Painting detail onto the petals

Putting the flower together

# poppy

The poppy is a very delicate flower and relatively easy to make. It normally appears around June and flowers into autumn. It is also the flower of remembrance as it grew on the battlefields of Flanders after the First World War.

## Materials

Green and red flowerpaste

Dusting powders (petal dust) in the following colours: black, red, foliage green

24- and 30-gauge wire

Edible glue

Seedhead stamens

Black sugartex

Light green florist's tape

Clear alcohol (gin or vodka)

## Equipment

Iceland poppy petal cutters (Fine Cut 518)

Poppy petal veiners (SK Great Impressions)

Daisy leaf cutters (Jem L4B)

Wire cutters

Small round-nosed pliers

Angled tweezers

Paintbrush

Ball tool

Jar or bottle

Craft knife

## Centre (seed pod)

**1** Take a piece of 24-gauge wire about 30 cm (12 in) long. Make a small hook at one end using round-nosed pliers. Shape a small piece of green flowerpaste into a cone. Dip the hooked end of the wire into edible glue and push into the pointed end of the cone. Flatten the top of the cone a little. Using a pair of angled tweezers, pinch lines into the top of the cone. They should resemble a cartwheel. Leave to dry.

## Stamens

**2** To make the stamens follow step 2, page 24. Paint the stamens using black dusting powder mixed with a little clear alcohol.

## Petals

**3** Cut a 30-cm (12-in) length of 30-gauge wire. Roll out a piece of red flowerpaste quite finely, leaving a ridge through the centre. Cut two small petals using poppy cutters and cover one with a plastic bag. Moisten the wire with edible glue and insert it into the ridge. Vein with a poppy veiner and transfer to a petal pad. Soften the edges using the ball tool.

Pinching lines into the top of the cone

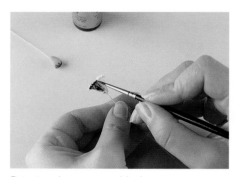
Painting the stamens black

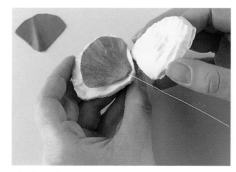
Veining the poppy petals

Hang upside down while you do the other petal. Leave to dry.

**4** Position the two petals opposite one another underneath the stamens and tape with pale green florist's tape.

**5** Take another piece of red paste and roll out thinly. Cut two large petals, vein and ball as before. Brush a little edible glue at the bottom and a very little up the edges. Stick these opposite one

Taping in the first two petals

Attaching the two back petals

Painting the base of the petals with black

another in the gaps. Place upright in a jar or bottle to dry.

**6** Carefully dust the flower with red powder. Paint four patches of black at the base of the petals. Steam and leave to dry.

## Buds

**7** Cut a piece of 24-gauge wire about 15 cm (6 in) long. Make a hook at one end. Take a smallish piece of green paste. Roll into an oval. Make a small cut all the way round lengthways with a craft knife. Dip the hooked end of the wire into

edible glue and attach to the bud. Use a craft knife to stab the surface all over to texture. Leave to dry then dust the cut line only with red . Dust the bud with foliage green. Twist one-third-width florist's tape down the stem from the bud, attach to flower stem several inches down.

## Leaves

**8** Poppy leaves are very delicate. They appear towards the bottom of the flower. Use the daisy leaf cutters to make basic leaves and dust with foliage green when dry. Steam and leave to dry.

# honeysuckle

Honeysuckle is so called because the nectar tastes like honey. These flowers have a wonderful scent and look beautiful in natural sprays. The silk stamens used here are tiny and need to be handled with great care. You will need several leaves, buds and flowers for each stem.

## Materials

Pale cream and green flowerpaste

Dusting powders (petal dust) in the
following colours: daffodil, spring
green, champagne, foliage green,
aubergine

28-gauge wire

Silk stamens

Light green florist's tape

## Equipment

Honeysuckle cutters (Orchard Products
HS1-HS3)

Periwinkle leaf cutters (Fine Cut 498)

Rose leaf veiners (SK Great
Impressions)

Wire cutters

Cel stick

Cocktail stick (toothpick) with one end
rounded off

Paintbrush

Craft knife

## Flowers

**1** Take a piece of 28-gauge wire 10 cm (4 in) long. Tape six stamens to this leaving one of them proud. Dust the lower stamens with daffodil and the proud one with spring green.

**2** Mould a piece of cream flowerpaste into a Mexican hat shape, making sure the point is very slender. Transfer to your board and roll the excess paste out thinly from the centre of the shape.

**3** Cut out the flower shape using the medium-sized cutter. Make a hole in the centre with a small Cel stick. Thin down top petals and tongue with a cocktail stick.

**4** Moisten the base of the stamens. Thread down the throat of the flower, leaving them protruding. Roll the back of the flower between your thumb and index finger to form a narrow tube. Bend the tongue of the top petals downwards. Leave to dry. Twist a narrow piece of tape below the

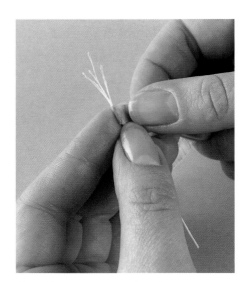

Attaching stamens to the wire

Making the Mexican hat shape

flowers to make the calyx. Dust with champagne.

## Buds

**5** Shape a small piece of cream flowerpaste into a slender teardrop. Moisten the end of a piece of 28-gauge wire with edible glue and insert it into the pointed end of the flowerpaste. Curve the bud slightly upwards and make five cuts lengthways. Leave to dry. Make the calyx and dust as for the flower (dust the small buds spring green).

## Leaves

**6** Use periwinkle leaf cutters to make the leaves and vein using rose leaf veiners. When all leaves are dry, dust with foliage green. Catch the very edges with aubergine.

## Assembly

**7** Start at the top with two little leaves. Tape down a little way. Add in another set, then add buds and flowers in pairs. Each set should have two leaves underneath them. Steam the completed stem and leave to dry.

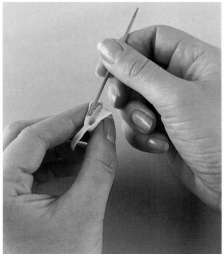

Cutting out the flower shape

Thinning down the top petals

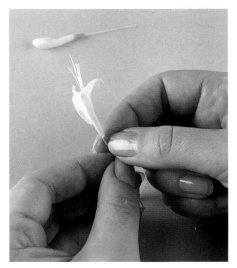

Attaching the calyx

# snowdrop

Snowdrops are one of the earliest of the spring flowers, appearing in January. They are easy to make and look lovely when presented in a clump with all their foliage.

## Materials

White and green flowerpaste

Dusting powders (petal dust) in the
  following colours: autumn green,
  foliage and lemon

26- and 28-gauge wire

Edible glue

Small white stamens

Yellow Sugartex

Clear alcohol (gin or vodka)

Light and dark green florist's tape

Gum glue

## Equipment

Snowdrop cutters set (Fine Cut 620)

Wire cutters

Small round-nosed pliers

Fine scissors

Paintbrush

Ball tool

Cocktail stick (toothpick) with one end
  rounded off

## Centre

**1** Take a piece of 28-gauge wire about 15 cm (6 in) long. Make a small hook at one end using round-nosed pliers. Roll a small piece of white flowerpaste into a ball about the size of a peppercorn. Moisten the wire with edible glue and insert into the ball. Cut three stamens down to about 4 mm ($1/4$ in). Moisten the ends and stick them into the ball. Brush with a little edible glue and dip into yellow Sugartex. Leave to dry.

## Petals

**2** Thinly roll a piece of white flowerpaste. Cut out the shape using the three-heart petals cutter. Using the small end of a ball tool, elongate and cup each section. Take the centre piece again and paint about one-third with edible glue. Insert the wire through the middle of the inner petals. Bring the petals down over the ball. The petals should not overlap. Leave to dry, then paint tiny lines with autumn green dusting powder mixed with alcohol along the bottom of the petals, following the outline of the petals.

**3** Roll out another piece of white flowerpaste. Cut out the outside petals. Elongate and cup as before. Moisten the centre with edible glue

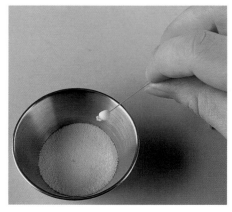

Dipping the stamens into Sugartex

Painting the petals

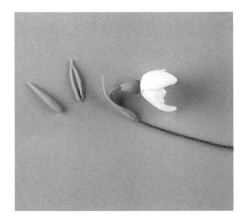

and thread the wire through the centre. Make sure the outer petals sit in between the gaps of the inside ones. Leave to dry.

## Ovary

**4** Take a piece of half-width light green tape. Tape down about 5 cm (2 in) down from the back of the flower. Roll a piece of green flowerpaste into an oval shape about the size of a peppercorn. Moisten the back of the flower with edible glue and push the ovary down the stem onto the flower.

## Spathe

**5** Roll a small piece of green flowerpaste into a sausage about 1 cm (¹/₂ in) long. Make one end quite pointed. Place on your board and, using a cocktail stick, press down along the length of the shape quite hard. The centre should be translucent. Bend the flower head down. Attach the spathe to the stem where the green tape ends. It will flop forwards to follow the shape of the stem. Leave to dry.

Using a piece of one-third-width dark green tape, tape down the rest of the stem from under the spathe.

## Leaves

**6** Make linear leaves (see page 14). They are normally in pairs with each flower. Attach two leaves, one either side of the flower with curve facing inwards. Steam and leave to dry.

Making the outer petals

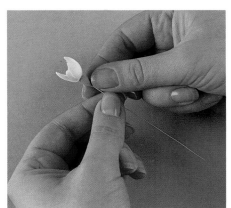

Positioning the ovary

Attaching the spathe

# periwinkle

This pretty mauve flower, which can also be white, appears in early spring and flowers well into May. It is an easy flower to make and quite quick too. It has two leaves to every flower or bud, so quite a lot of foliage is required.

## Materials

White, yellow and green flowerpaste

Dusting powders (petal dust) in the following colours: lavender, cornflower, foliage green, aubergine

28-gauge wire

Edible glue

One-third-strength confectioner's glaze

Light green florist's tape

## Equipment

Periwinkle cutter (PME LP 451)

Periwinkle leaf cutters (Fine Cut 498)

Ivy leaf veiners succinata (SK Great Impressions)

Wire cutters

Small round-nosed pliers

Wooden dowel cut into a pentagon at one end

Ball tool

Cocktail stick (toothpick) with one end rounded off

Cotton wool

Paintbrush

Tweezers

Craft knife

Fine scissors

## Flower

**1** Take a piece of 28-gauge wire about 8 cm (3 in) long. Hook it at one end using round-nosed pliers. Take a piece of white flowerpaste and make into a Mexican hat shape. Cut out one shape using the periwinkle cutter.

**2** Use a shaped dowel to make a hole in the centre of the flower. Place the flower on a petal pad and lengthen each petal with a ball tool. Transfer to a board and, making a slight point at one tip, widen each petal with a cocktail stick.

**3** Dip the hooked end of the wire into a little edible glue. Pull it through the middle of the flower. Roll the back of the flower between your thumb and index finger to make a slender tube. Leave to dry.

**4** Place a small piece of cotton wool in the centre of the flower. Mix together lavender and cornflower dusting powders and dust the back and front, leaving a little white showing at the stem end. Remove the cotton wool.

**5** Roll a tiny piece of yellow flowerpaste into a ball. Moisten the centre of the flower using a little edible glue. Drop the ball of paste

Creating the periwinkle flower shape

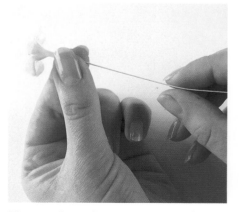

Thinning down the back of the flower

into the flower centre using a pair of tweezers. Press down with the shaped dowel. Make five tiny cuts in the paste ball with a craft knife. Steam the flower and leave to dry.

## Calyx

**6** Cut a piece of florist's tape to about 1 cm ($^1/_2$ in) long. Cut out five points from the tape. Wrap it around the base of the flower.

## Buds

**7** Cut a piece of 28-gauge wire to 8 cm (3 in) long. Shape a small piece of white flowerpaste into a slender cone. Dip the wire into edible glue and insert into the cone.

**8** Use a craft knife to cut five lines lengthways into the cone to represent the petals. Leave to dry. Dust using lavender and cornflower mixed together. Make the calyx as for the flower and secure at the base of the bud then steam and dry.

## Leaves

**9** Make several pairs of leaves using the periwinkle leaf cutters and ivy veiners. Dust with foliage green, steam and leave to dry, then glaze with one-third-strength confectioner's varnish.

## Assembly

**10** Take a pair of leaves and tape together using one-third-width tape. Work down the stem adding in the buds and flowers. There should be two leaves to each flower or bud.

Dusting the petals

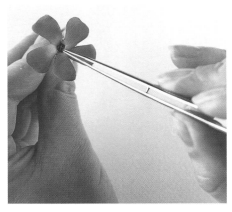

Positioning the centre of the flower

Wrapping the calyx round the flower

# cherry blossom

This is the earliest of the blossoms and one of the most delicate. The leaves come later so you only need to make the flowers.

## Materials

Pale pink and green flowerpaste

Dusting powders (petal dust) in the following colours: spring green, lemon, pink, white, foliage green, burgundy

22- and 28-gauge wire

Silk stamens

Edible glue

Hi-tack non-toxic glue

Cornflour (cornstarch)

Light green and brown florist's tape

## Equipment

Stephanotis cutter (Tinkertech 568)

Calyx cutter (Tinkertech 406)

Wire cutters

Cocktail stick (toothpick) with one end rounded off

Ball tool

Small Cel stick

Fine scissors

Craft knife

## Centre

**1** Use the same technique for gluing the stamens as for the open rose, step 2, page 24. However, as there is no middle piece, just glue the small bundles straight onto a shortish length of 28-gauge wire. Leave one proud and dust this with spring green. Dust the others with lemon and leave the threads white.

## Petals

**2** Take a small piece of pale pink flowerpaste and roll into a Mexican hat shape. Using the stephanotis cutter, cut one shape. Take a nick from the tip of each petal, using one of the points of the cutter.

Cutting a nick from the tip of the petal

**3** Dust your index finger with cornflour. Lay each petal in turn down on your finger, and using the rounded end of a cocktail stick, thin each petal.

**4** Moisten the bottom of the stamens with a little edible glue. Make a small hole in the centre of the flower. Thread the flower up the wire and secure, leaving the stamens proud. Leave to dry. Dust the petals edges with a mixture of pink and white.

## Calyx

**5** Shape a piece of pale green flowerpaste into a Mexican hat. Keeping the back very slender and

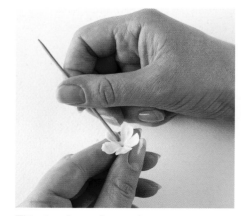

Thinning down the petals

quite narrow, cut out the calyx using the calyx cutter. Place onto a petal pad and use a ball tool to elongate each sepal. Make a small hole in the centre of the calyx using the pointed end of a Cel stick.

**6** Moisten the centre of the calyx with edible glue. Thread this up the wire and secure behind the flower. Dust the outside of the calyx with a mixture of foliage and spring green. Dust a little burgundy onto the calyx.

## Buds

**7** Take a small piece of pale pink flowerpaste about the size of a peppercorn. Roll into a cone shape then slightly taper at both ends. Make three cuts lengthways using a craft knife. Moisten the end of a small length of 28-gauge wire with edible glue. Insert into the bottom of the bud. Leave to dry. Dust with pink. Make the calyx as above, and attach under the bud.

## Assembly

**8** Tape the stems under the buds and the flowers, then in turn tape these into bunches of three or five flowers and buds. Add in a length of 22-gauge wire.

**9** For each little bunch you need to make another calyx. Do the same process as for the flowers and buds, only cut off the points, thread these up behind each bunch and secure with edible glue. Dust with foliage green and burgundy.

**10** Make a cluster of buds at the top then tape in assorted bud and flower clusters using brown tape, until the stem length required is achieved. Dust the whole stem with a little foliage green. Steam and leave to dry.

Dusting the petals

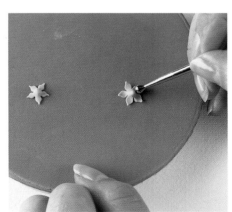

Elongating the sepals of the calyx

Attaching the calyx to the flower

# cyclamen

Cyclamen can be found in shades of pale to dark pink, red and white and there are large and small varieties. It flowers in the autumn and goes on flowering into early spring.

## Materials

Pink, green and brown flowerpaste

Dusting powders (petal dust) in the following colours: pink, burgundy, forest green, eucalyptus

24- and 28-gauge wire

Edible glue

Beige florist's tape

Stamens

Clear alcohol (gin or vodka)

## Equipment

Calyx cutter (Tinkertech 406)

Freesia cutter (AP Cutters F62)

Leaf serrator (AP Cutters)

Nasturtium leaf veiners (SK Great Impressions)

Wire cutters

Small round-nosed pliers

Paintbrush

Craft knife

Cocktail stick (toothpick) with one end rounded off

Dresden tool

Cotton wool buds

## Flower

**1** Cut a piece of 24-gauge wire about 15 cm (6 in) long. Make a hook at one end using round-nosed pliers. Shape a small piece of pink flowerpaste into a cone and hollow out. It needs to be about $1/2$ cm ($1/4$ in) wide. Moisten the hooked end of the wire with edible glue. Pull through the cone to embed the hook.

**2** Roll out a small piece of green flowerpaste quite finely. Cut one shape using the calyx cutter. Brush with edible glue and position onto the back of the cone. Tape with one-third-width tape twice to thicken. Use the pliers to bend the wire into an S shape so the cup is upwards. Leave to dry thoroughly.

**3** Cut two shapes using the freesia cutter. Cut away the sides of the petals with a craft knife to make them more pointed. Use the blunt end of a cocktail stick where it begins to thicken to re-shape the petal. Work on each side to thin down and widen, keeping the centre slightly thicker. If there is still a point at the top, trim this away.

**4** Place the petals on a petal pad. Using the narrow end of a dresden tool, mark lines downwards from the petals to give the impression that they are separate. Cut the triangular piece at the bottom away.

**5** Paint the bottom of the shape with edible glue approximately 1 cm ($1/2$ in). Secure this into the cone next to the wire, pushing it gently with a cocktail stick to secure. Make sure the petals are stuck to both the inside and the outside of the cone. Give the petals a little twist. Put to one side with petal hanging down.

**6** Take the second petal shape. Cut away one petal then trim and shape as before. Secure these with the

Bending the wire into an S shape

deep. Gently roll the bud between your thumb and index finger. Then twist the whole thing from its point. Roll another piece of green flowerpaste, cut out another calyx. Soften the edges with a ball tool. Brush with edible glue and secure on the rounded end of the cone.

## Leaves

**10** Use the templates on page 78 to cut out cyclamen leaf shapes. Cut lengths of 28-gauge wire. These don't need to be too long. Cover using one-third-width beige tape. Moisten the wire with edible glue then insert into the ridge of the leaf Using the leaf serrator, cut away at the edge of the leaves to create an uneven edge. Vein using a nasturtium leaf veiner and very carefully bend the wire into a gentle curve in the leaf, then bend the stalk down so it's nearly at right angles to the leaf. Allow to dry. Dust the leaves with forest green then, using a cotton wool bud with a little alcohol, lift off the green in patches. Leave to dry. Mix forest green and eucalyptus and dust over where you have lifted the colour to create the pattern. Catch the edges with burgundy powder. Scratch very fine lines away with a needle. Steam and leave to dry.

other petals on the other side of the wire. Twist to shape and leave to dry.

**7** Straighten the wire out and carefully dust with pink. To create a deeper ring of colour around the bottom, paint on the powder then, with a clean, damp brush, brush upwards to soften the line. Brush a little burgundy dusting powder from the bottom of the stem upwards (the colour fades nearer the top).

**8** Shape a tiny piece of brown flowerpaste into a cone. Secure this into the centre of the flower, then push in a short piece of stamen

thread. This protrudes about 2 mm (1/8 in) below the rim.

## Buds

**9** Cut a piece of 28-gauge wire shorter than for the flower. Make a hook at one end and tape with one-third-width florist's tape. Shape a piece of pink flowerpaste into a slender pointed cone. The buds vary in size, but don't make them too big – around 1.5 cm (1/2 in) would be the largest. Moisten the hooked end of the wire with edible glue and insert into the bottom of the cone. Using the craft knife, make five lines length-ways. These need to be quite

Shaping the petals

Attaching the petals to the cone

Dusting the flower with colour

# anemone

The anemone appears in spring and can be in red, purple or bright pink. The stamens of the anemone are normally the same colour as the flower. There is also a white variety that has a green centre.

## Materials

White and green flowerpaste

Dusting powders (petal dust) in the following colours: your choice for the flower, plus violet

22-, 28- and 30-gauge wires

Very fine silk or cotton thread in either cream or white

Light green florist's tape

Black Sugartex

## Equipment

Anemone petal cutters (Fine Cut 107 or Tinkertech leaf set 225-228)

Christmas rose petal veiners (SK Great Impressions)

Daisy leaf cutters (Jem L4B)

Wire cutters

Fine scissors

Emery board

Paintbrush

Craft knife

Ball tool

White kitchen towel, torn into 5-mm (¹/4 in) strips

Dresden tool

## Stamens and centre

**1** Take a 15-cm (6-in) long piece of 30-gauge wire and bend it in half. Holding the bend, twist the wire to make a small loop.

**2** Wind fine silk or cotton thread around two slightly parted fingers 70-80 times. Remove from your fingers and twist to make a figure of eight. Fold this in half to make a smaller loop.

**3** Attach the wire to the cotton with the loop facing in. (Attach another piece of 30-gauge wire on the opposite side to make a second stamen.) Secure by twisting the wire

and then taping over the base of the cotton and down the wire with half-width florist's tape. You should still be able to see the loop in the centre. Cut the thread in half and trim off a little.

**4** Holding the stamens between your thumb and index finger, rub the tips with an emery board. Dust all over with dusting powder in your chosen colour.

**5** Mix some black Sugartex with violet dusting powder to make pollen. Brush some edible glue onto the tips of the threads and dip these into the pollen mixture.

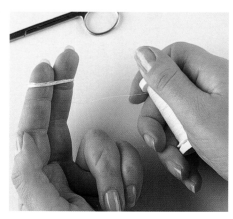

Winding thread for the stamens

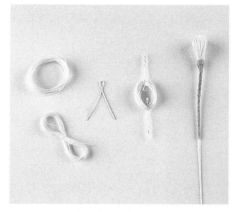

The stages of making the stamens

**6** Roll a small piece of white flowerpaste into a ball. Place this onto a piece of wire. Texture the surface with a craft knife, paint with edible glue and dip into the pollen mix. Remove the ball from the wire.

**7** Open the centre of the stamens up with the handle of a paintbrush. Paint edible glue on the centre loop and place the ball into position on this. Allow to dry.

## Petals
**8** Cut between 9 and 15 pieces of 30-gauge wire, each approximately 15 cm (6 in) long.

Placing the flower centre in the stamens

**9** Roll a piece of white flowerpaste out thinly, leaving a small ridge through the centre. Cut out a petal shape using the anemone cutters. Insert a moistened 30-gauge wire into the ridge and vein with the Christmas rose petal veiner.

**10** Soften the edges of the petal using a ball tool. Using the larger end, cup the petal slightly. When the petal is nearly dry, dust with your chosen colour, leaving a white patch at the bottom. Steam and then leave to dry. Re-dust and steam.

This gives a much stronger colour. When dry, if any colour has gone onto the white area scratch it away carefully using the point of the craft knife. Repeat steps 9-10 to make 9-15 petals, using the various anemone petal cutters.

**11** Tape a piece of 22-gauge wire under the stamens using half-width light green tape. Tape the smaller petals in first, spreading them around the centre. Continue taping

Dusting the petal

in the other petals, using the larger ones for the outside.

**12** To thicken the stem, wrap a piece of kitchen roll around the wire from under the petals downwards. Tape over this with full-width tape.

## Leaves

**13** Roll out a piece of green flowerpaste, leaving a ridge through the centre. Cut out a leaf shape using a daisy leaf cutter, then cut away the bottom leaving three sections.

**14** Cut a piece of 28-gauge wire 5 cm (2 in) long. Moisten the end with edible glue and insert into the ridge, making sure it goes right to the tip of the leaf. On a petal pad broaden each leaf section using the small end of the ball tool, then use a pair of scissors to cut away little V shapes from the edges of the leaves. Re-soften the edges and vein one line lengthways from each section using a dresden tool.

**15** Dust the leaf before it has dried, using foliage green with a little aubergine around the edges. Return the leaf to the pad and ball it a little to give some movement. Leave to dry. Repeat this two or three more times. Each flower needs three to four leaves. When dry, steam lightly. Tape the leaves to the stem, leaving a gap of about 2¹/₂ cm (1 in) from the flower head.

## Buds

**16** Make a small hook at the end of a piece of 22-gauge wire 10 cm (4 in) long using round-nosed pliers. Roll a piece of white flowerpaste into a ball. Moisten the hooked end of wire with edible glue and insert into the ball. Leave to dry.

**17** Roll a piece of white flowerpaste quite thinly. Cut out three to five petals using the smallest petal cutter. Vein using the Christmas rose veiner. On the pad, soften the petal edges using the ball tool. Dust petals on both sides using your chosen colour. Use edible glue

to stick the petals onto the centre ball. Make sure they don't look like a rosebud. Pinch the tops a little to heighten at the top. Leave to dry then re-dust and steam. Leave to dry again.

**18** Make smaller leaves as before, only this time attach them immediately under the petals.

# sweet pea

The sweet pea is a very popular, scented flower that arrives in summer. Its colour range includes white, cream, pinks, lilacs and purples. It also makes a good cut flower.

## Materials

White and green flowerpaste

Dusting powders (petal dust) in the following colours: mimosa, spring green, white, colour of your choice for the main flower, foliage green

24-, 26-, 28- and 30-gauge wire

Edible glue

Light green florist's tape

Half-strength confectioner's glaze

## Equipment

Sweet pea cutters (Tinkertech 555-556)

Rose petal cutters (Tinkertech 276-280)

Small calyx cutter (Orchard Products R13)

Leaf cutters (Tinkertech leaf 225-228)

Single peony leaf veiners (SK Great Impressions, 5-cm)

Wire cutters

Small round-nosed pliers

Craft knife

Ceramic silk veining tool (Holly products)

Cocktail stick (toothpick) with one end rounded off

Dresden tool

Paintbrush

Small Cel stick

Ball tool

## Keel (centre)

**1** Take a piece of 24-gauge wire about 15 cm (6 in) long. Make a hook at one end using round-nosed pliers. Roll a small piece of white flowerpaste into a teardrop shape. Make a slight point at both ends. Flatten the shape a little. It should look like a Cornish pasty. Moisten the wire hook with edible glue and insert into the base of the shape. Pinch the edge of the rounded part to make it angular. Indent this using a craft knife and open slightly. Curve the straight edge back gently.

## Petals

**2** First make the wing petals. Cut two 15-cm (6-in) pieces of 30-gauge wire. Roll a piece of white flowerpaste leaving a ridge down the middle. This only needs to be halfway and should not be too obvious. Cut out two petals using the sweet pea cutter, making sure you have a left and a right. Cover one with a plastic bag. Moisten the end of a wire and insert into the ridge. Pinch to secure.

**3** Place the petal ridge-side-up on

your board and vein using a silk veining tool. Keep the point of the tool at the point of the petal, rolling it backwards and forwards. Soften and frill the edges using a cocktail stick. Repeat with the other petal. Leave to dry for a short time until firm. Tape the two wing petals to the keel, using one-third-width florist's tape. The longest side of the petal should be upwards.

**4** To make the back petal cut a 15-cm (6-in) piece of 28-gauge wire. Roll another piece of white flowerpaste leaving a ridge through the middle. Cut out a petal with the

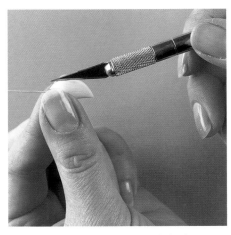

Indenting the keel with a craft knife

Attaching the wing petals to the keel

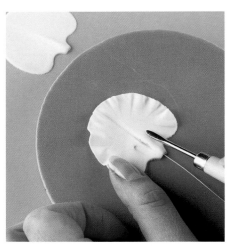

Making indentations with a dresden tool

Making the calyx to complete the flower

cutter. Moisten the wire with edible glue and insert into the ridge. Do not push it up too high.

**5** Vein and frill as for the wing petals. Place the petal on a petal pad and, using the fine end of a dresden tool, make a central vein downwards. Turn the petal over. Use the broad end to make two hollows either side of the central vein at the base of the petal.

**6** Tape the back petal tightly in behind the wings. Squeeze the base of the petals together. Curve the back petal backwards slightly. Allow to dry before dusting.

**7** Mix a little mimosa, spring green and white dusting powder together. Carefully dust the tip of the keel and the base of the petals. Dust the petals with the colour of your choice, starting at the edge and working inwards.

## Calyx

**8** Take a small piece of green flowerpaste. Shape into a Mexican hat, keeping the back very slender.

Place on your board and thin down the flat area with a small Cel stick. Cut out the calyx using a small calyx cutter. On the petal pad, elongate each section using the small end of a ball tool. Hollow out the centre of each section using the broad end of a dresden tool. Make a hole in the centre of the calyx using the pointed end of the cel stick. Brush a little edible glue in the centre and thread onto the back of the flower. Secure the three sections at the back. Curl the two at the front down slightly. Dust with foliage green.

**9** Using one-third-width florist's tape, tape down the stem. Leave to dry. Bend the stem using the round-nosed pliers. Hold the stem close behind the calyx and use your other hand to pull the wire down. This will give a nice curve. Steam and leave to dry.

## Buds

**10** Make the keel as for the flowers, only a little smaller. Roll a piece of white flowerpaste quite finely and cut out two shapes using the two smallest rose petal cutters.

Using a pair of sharp scissors cut a narrow V shape from one of the petals. Vein using a ceramic veining tool. Soften the edges with a cocktail stick. Brush edible glue at the base of the petal and attach to the back edge of the keel.

**11** Vein and frill the larger shape. Mark in a central vein using a dresden tool. Attach over the top of the first petal. Squeeze the base of the petals to secure. Curl the back petal outwards, attach the calyx and dust. Steam and leave to dry.

## Leaves

**12** Make pairs of leaves using the leaf cutters. When dry dust with foliage green, steam and leave to dry.

## Bracts

**13** Cut lengths of 30-gauge wire about 4 cm (1¹/₂ in) long. Shape a small piece of green flowerpaste into a teardrop and insert a moistened wire. Flatten the shape by rolling with a small rolling pin. Cut out a spear shape with scissors. Vein a central line with a dresden

tool and soften the edges with a ball tool. Leave to dry and dust with foliage green.

## Tendrils

**14** Cut several pieces of half-width tape. Twist these into long needles. Tape three of these together onto a 26-gauge wire. Twist the tops around a Cel stick to give them a little bend. Add the tendrils down the stem in pairs.

## Assembly

**15** Tape flowers and buds into small groups with the buds at the top and flowers underneath. The flowers and leaves are separate but it looks effective when they are displayed together.

# winter aconite

Like the snowdrop, the aconite is an early flower. A bright yellow buttercup-like flower, it is easy enough to make but its unusual leaves are very delicate.

## Materials

Yellow and green flowerpaste

Dusting powders (petal dust) in the following colours: primrose, leaf green, foliage green

26-gauge wire and thin uncovered wire

Cream cotton

Light green florist's tape

Edible glue

Yellow Sugartex

Clear alcohol (gin or vodka)

## Equipment

Six-petal flower cutter (Orchard Products N6)

Snowdrop cutter (Fine Cut 620)

Daisy cutter (Orchard Products DY1)

Fine scissors

Wire cutters

Cocktail stick (toothpick) with one end rounded off

Paintbrush

Ball tool

Craft knife

## Stamens

**1** Wind cream cotton thread around two fingers about 50 times. Remove from your fingers. Attach a small piece of uncovered florist's wire at each end of the cotton and twist to secure. Cut the cotton in half. You now have two centres. Take a piece of one-third-width tape and a piece of 26-gauge wire approximately 10 cm (4 in) long. Tape the cottons to the wire ensuring the actual bottom of the cotton is taped as well as the rest of the wire. Use a paintbrush to moisten the cotton tips only with edible glue and dip into yellow Sugartex.

**2** Take a piece of yellow flowerpaste and cut out one shape using the six-petal flower cutter. Broaden each section with a cocktail stick. Paint a little edible glue onto the centre of each section. Bring the edges of each petal together. When all six petals are done, push the shape onto the wire and secure behind the stamens.

## Petals

**3** Roll out a smallish piece of yellow flowerpaste quite thinly. Cut out one shape using the back piece of a snowdrop cutter. Elongate and slightly widen. Transfer to a petal

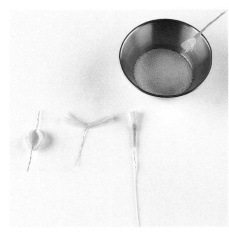

Texturing the centre of the flower

Pushing the six-petal shape onto the wire

pad and cup each petal inwards with a ball tool. Moisten the petal centre with edible glue and slide them up the wire behind the centre.

**4** Roll another piece of yellow flowerpaste, this time leaving it a little thicker. Cut another shape using the same cutter. Elongate and broaden to around half the width again. Cup as before. Moisten the centre with edible glue and attach to the back of the flower. Secure with petals sitting in between the first layer. Leave to dry.

**5** Carefully dust the petals with primrose. Use leaf green sparingly in the middle, but do not dust the stamens. Steam and leave to dry. Mix a little leaf green powder with alcohol and paint very faint lines inside the petals.

## Calyx

**6** Roll a piece of green flowerpaste. Cut out one shape using the large daisy cutter. Using a craft knife, make two or three cuts lengthways in each section. Using the craft knife or sharp scissors cut each section to a point. Broaden each of

these with a cocktail stick. Dust with foliage green immediately. Moisten the back of the flower with edible glue and attach the calyx cup behind

it. Fiddle around with the calyx so it hangs a little unevenly – this will make it look more realistic. Steam and leave to dry.

Cupping the petals

Putting together the flower

Making the calyx

63

# clematis

There are many varieties of clematis with very varied structures. Some have four petals, some six and others have many more. Some are even bell-shaped. They tend to come in white, pinks, blues and purple shades, but there are also yellow ones.

## Materials

Cream, pale mauve and green flowerpaste

Dusting powders (petal dust) in the following colours: spring green, red, empress purple, mauve mist, foliage green, eucalyptus

Cream cotton

24-, 26- and 28-gauge wire and uncovered wire

Cream cotton

Light green florist's tape

Edible glue

Yellow Sugartex

## Equipment

Bauhinia cutters (Fine Cut 156c)

Clematis veiners (SK Great Impressions)

Leaf cutters (Tinkertech leaf set 225-228)

Clematis leaf veiners (SK Great Impressions)

Wire cutters

Craft knife

Paintbrush

Ball tool

Small round-nosed pliers

## Stamens

**1** Wind cream cotton thread around two fingers about 20 times. Continue to make the stamens following step 1, page 62, only do not dip the stamens in Sugartex. Dust the tips of the stamens with red dusting powder.

**2** Take a small piece of cream flowerpaste and roll into a thin strip. Use a craft knife to cut lines downwards about 1 mm from the bottom of the paste. Place on a petal pad and ball the tips to make them curl inwards. Moisten the uncut edge with edible glue and wrap around the stamens. Hang upside down till nearly dry, then turn back up the right way so they fan out a little. These are very delicate so you need to take care. Dust a little spring green into the centre of the flower.

## Petals

**3** Cut six pieces of 28-gauge wire about 8 cm (3 in) long. Roll a piece of pale mauve paste leaving a ridge through the centre. Cut out one petal shape using the bauhinia cutter. Insert a wire moistened with edible glue into the bottom of the petal and vein using the clematis veiner. Transfer to a petal pad and soften the edges with a ball tool. Curve forwards. Leave to dry. Repeat with the remaining petals.

Making the flower centres with cotton

Cutting vertical lines into the flowerpaste

**4** Dust the petals with empress purple. Work from the edges inwards leaving a pale area through the centre. Dust this area with mauve mist. Dust the very tips and base with spring green. Do the back the same with the green, but just work from the outside edges in a little way with the empress purple.

**5** Take three petals and tape them around the stamens using one-third-width green tape. Add the other three petals underneath in the gaps in the same way.

## Buds

**6** Cut a piece of 24-gauge wire and make a hook at one end using round-nosed pliers. Form a piece of green flowerpaste into a tapered cone. Make six cuts lengthways to represent petals. Dip the hooked end of the wire into edible glue and insert into the bulbous end of the bud. Give the bud a gentle twist and leave to dry. Dust with foliage green and a little eucalyptus over the top.

## Leaves

**7** Make the leaves using green flowerpaste. Clematis have quite a lot of leaves and they are normally in sets of three.

## Assembly

**8** Take a bud and tape the stem using one-third-width tape. Add in two sets of leaves. Tape down a little further. Add another two sets of leaves and a flower. Carry on until the length of stem is achieved. Steam and leave to dry.

The different petal stages

Attaching the first row of petals

Attaching a bud to the flower

65

# acorn & oak

The English oak bears green acorns and foliage in spring and summer, and turns to browns and golds in autumn so can be made in either colour.

## Materials

Cream flowerpaste

Dusting powders (petal dust) in the following colours: copper, russet, nutkin brown

24-, 26- and 28-gauge wire

Edible glue

Small cream stamens

Brown florist's tape

Half-strength confectioner's glaze

## Equipment

Acorn cup mould, optional (Sugar City)

Oak leaf cutters (Orchard Products OL1-OL4)

Oak leaf veiner (SK Great Impressions)

Wire cutters

Small round-nosed pliers

Paintbrush

Tweezers

Ball tool

Cocktail stick (toothpick) or nutmeg grater

## Acorn

**1** Take a piece of 26-gauge wire approximately 10 cm (4 in) long. Make a small hook at one end using round-nosed pliers. Form a smallish piece of cream flowerpaste into an egg shape. Moisten the hooked end of the wire with edible glue and insert into one end of the shape. Use tweezers to stick a small cream stamen at the other end. Leave to dry.

**2** Dust with assorted brown powders, steam and leave to dry. Glaze with half-strength confectioner's glaze.

**3** Roll another smaller piece of cream flowerpaste into a ball using the small end of a ball tool. Hollow out to make a cup and thin down the edges of the cup. Alternatively, use an acorn cup mould.

**4** Brush the base of the acorn with edible glue. Push the cup up underneath. Gently mould the cup to fit neatly. Texture the cup by either pricking it all over with the sharp end of a cocktail stick or rolling it along a nutmeg grater.

**5** When dry, dust the cup with assorted brown dusting powders, making it slightly darker than the

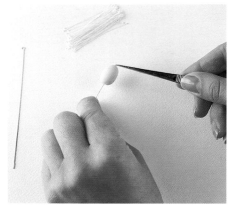

Placing a stamen in the acorn

Glazing the acorn

acorn. Dust the stamen with nutkin brown. Steam and leave to dry.

## Leaves

**6** Make oak leaves using the oak leaf cutters and veiners. When dry dust with various shades of brown. Steam and leave to dry.

Alternatively acorns or oak leaves can be made in shades of green.

## Assembly

**7** Tape the acorns singly or in pairs with leaves round them. Tape down the stems with one-third width brown tape.

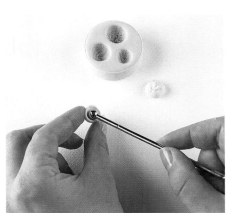

Thinning down the edges of the cup

Texturing the cup with a cocktail stick

Dusting the cup

# forget-me-not

These delicate little flowers are found wild in North America, Europe and New Zealand. The plant has thin stems with tiny flowers that are only 5 mm (¹/4 in) across.

## Materials

White, pale blue, yellow and green
flowerpaste
Dusting powders (petal dust) in the
following colours: bluebell, white,
foliage green, African violet
Edible glue
Light green florist's tape
28-, 30- and 33-gauge wire

## Equipment

Blossom plunger cutters (PME set of 3)
Chrysanthemum petal cutters
(Tinkertech 786, 785, 784)
Dresden tool
Wire cutters
Cocktail stick (toothpick)
Ball tool
Paintbrush
Craft knife

## Flowers

**1** Cut several lengths of 30-gauge wire approximately 2.5 cm (1 in) long. Take a tiny piece of yellow flowerpaste and shape it into a long cone. Hollow this out using the pointed end of a cocktail stick. Attach this to a wire end moistened with edible glue. Redefine the hole with a cocktail stick. Leave to dry.

**2** Roll a piece of blue flowerpaste out very finely. Using the smallest blossom cutter, cut out one shape. Place the shape on a petal pad and ball each petal gently with a ball tool. Paint a line of edible glue just around the top edge of the

hollowed cone on the wire. Slide the flower shape up the wire to the glue and secure. Leave to dry.

**3** Dust the flowers using bluebell mixed with a little white dusting powder. Do both the back of the petals and the front, being careful to leave a ring of yellow in the centre.

## Buds

**4** Take tiny pieces of white flowerpaste and make them into cone shapes. Attach the pointed end of each one to a 33-gauge wire moistened with edible glue. Mark a few lines lengthways with a craft knife to represent petals. Leave to

Redefining the hole with a cocktail stick

Securing the petal shapes to the wire

dry. Dust with bluebell mixed with a little African violet.

## Leaves

**5** Make leaves using the chrysanthemum petal cutters and vein one central line lengthways using a dresden tool.

## Assembly

**6** Using one-quarter-width tape, tape the buds closely together going down the stem. Start to add in the flowers. If the stem starts to get too thick, cut out a piece of wire. Add in the leaves in pairs and other stems of flowers as required.

Taping in the buds

Adding the flowers

**7** Carefully dust the stem including the yellow piece behind the flowers with foliage green. Catch a tiny bit at the base of the buds too. Steam gently and leave to dry.

# natural spray

Natural sprays are probably the easiest to do as you are only using one type of flower. The aim is simply to create something that is aesthetically pleasing, rather than something that follows a specific design. The flowers used in this spray are periwinkle – this is an ideal flower as it is a natural meanderer. Periwinkle leaves grow in pairs then the bud and flowers appear further down the stem, with one leaf either side of the flower or bud.

Taping in a flower between two leaves

Taping two sprays together

Adding the third and fourth sprays

### You will need

4 periwinkle sprays (see page 50)

Wire cutters

Light green florist's tape

Fine scissors

Perspex disk

A little royal icing

**1** Start by making up your periwinkle sprays. Take two small leaves and tape them together. Tape them down a little way and then add in another pair of leaves and a bud. Continue taping and then add two more leaves and a flower.

NOTE

You can vary the length of the sprays by adding more sets of leaves at the top before you start adding in the buds and flowers. Remember to start with the smaller leaves, adding the larger ones as you go further down the stem.

**2** Take two of the flower sprays and join them together near the bottom of the stem by taping with half-width florist's tape. Repeat with the other two sprays.

**3** Join the two pieces together by securing near the bottom with half-width florist's tape. Still holding the spray in one hand, bend the wire back at a right angle with your other hand. Tweak the flower stems so that they lie where you want them to go. Trim away any excess wire, leaving about 8 cm (3 in). Secure the flowers to a perspex disk with a little royal icing and position on your cake.

# posy

The Victorian posy is a popular shape for wedding bouquets – particularly for bridesmaids so this would make an ideal arrangement for a wedding cake. This traditional arrangement is simple to put together.

## You will need

4 pale yellow rose stems (see page 26)

3 pale yellow carnation stems (see page 22)

9 sprays of dried gypsophila (see note)

6 rose leaf sprays, each comprising 3 leaves (see page 27)

Wire cutters

Light green florist's tape

Fine scissors

Posy pick

## Note on gypsophila

Dried gypsophila is very useful as a filler in flower sprays and arrangements. It is available in bunches with each stem bearing a number of florets. Simply cut off each floret and attach to a piece of 30-gauge wire using one-third-width florist's tape. Steam the gypsophila lightly to open up the flowers. Gypsophila is usually used in its natural state but you can also colour the flowers. Simply dust with your chosen colour and then steam.

Taping the roses together

Adding the carnations

**1** Take one of the four roses and hold upright. Using one-third-width florist's tape, tape the other three roses around the central rose, making sure that they are evenly spaced.

**2** Take three sprays of gypsophila and tape them in between the gaps. Take one carnation, make a slight bend in the wire near the flower head and position the carnation in one of the spaces. Tape in underneath the gypsophila. Repeat with the other two carnations, making sure they are evenly spaced.

**3** Tape in the other six sprays of gypsophila evenly around. Finally take three sets of leaves and tape round at equal intervals. Secure the other sets of leaves in the spaces in

Taping in the sets of leaves

between using florist's tape. Trim the wires to about 8 cm (3 in).

**4** Decide where to position the spray on the cake, push in the posy pick and place the flowers in this.

# teardrop spray

This is a very popular spray design as it is an attractive oval shape that still looks quite natural but it will 'drape' nicely over a cake. I've used clematis which works really well – the strong colours of the flowers make a real impact on the cake.

Adding the first flower

Adding more leaves and flowers

Securing the final flower

## You will need

4 clematis flowers (see page 64)

6 sets of foliage, 2 with buds (see page 64)

Wire cutters

Light green florist's tape

Fine scissors

Posy pick

**1** Clematis leaves are usually found in sets of three. Take a spray of leaves and tape in a bud towards the middle of the leaves but slightly off centre. Add an opening flower and secure.

**2** Position two more flowers into the spray, one to the left and the other to the right and then add two more leaf sprays, one with a bud and one without, again positioning them to the left and right. Tape to secure.

**3** Secure the last flower centrally at the back of the spray but slightly lower than the others. Tape the final three leaf sprays in, one behind the flower and the other two to the right and left of the middle one. The leaves will slightly widen the back of the spray. Trim away any excess wire, leaving about 8 cm (3 in). Decide where to position the spray on the cake. Teardrop sprays usually drape over the side of the cake. Push in the posy pick and place the flowers in position.

# crescent spray

The crescent spray is a slightly more formal shape that works well for celebration cakes. Here I have used a pale yellow open rose which contrasts nicely with the dark green ivy leaves.

Taping two rosebud sprays together

Adding ivy sprays

Taping in the final ivy leaves

## You will need

1 open rose (see page 24)

4 rose buds (see page 24)

4 sets of rose leaves (see page 24)

2 sets of ivy with buds (see page 38)

3 small bunches of ivy (see page 38)

Wire cutters

Florist's tape

Fine scissors

Perspex disk

Small amount of royal icing

**1** Take one of the sets of rose leaves and tape one bud to the leaf spray, about one-third of the way down the stem. Repeat with the remaining leaf sprays and buds to make four small sprays. Take two of the sprays and tape these together, one slightly below the other. Repeat with the other two sprays. Gently bend one down to the right and one down to the left.

**2** Add a sprig of ivy with berries and a small bunch of leaves to each rose leaf spray. Secure in place by taping with florist's tape. You should now have the two tail ends of the crescent shape. Take one of the

sprays and bend the wire backwards at an angle, repeat with the other spray.

**3** Take the rose and tape to one of the leaf and ivy 'tails'. Position the second leaf and ivy spray on the other side of the rose and secure. Tape in a final set of ivy leaves at the top of the crescent, just above the rose. Trim away any excess wire so you are left with about 8 cm (3 in). Attach to a perspex disk with a little royal icing and position on your cake.

# templates

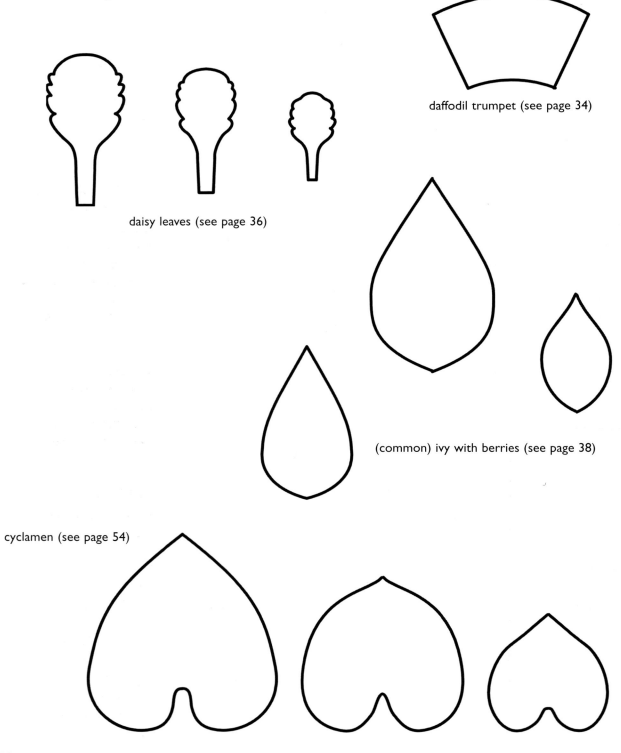

daffodil trumpet (see page 34)

daisy leaves (see page 36)

(common) ivy with berries (see page 38)

cyclamen (see page 54)

# useful addresses

## UK

**AP Cutters**
Treelands
Hillside Road
Bleadon, Weston-Super-Mare
North Somerset BA24 0AA
Tel/fax: 01934 812787

**Cel Cakes and Cel Crafts**
Springfield House
Gate Helmsley
York YO41 1NF
Tel: 01759 371447
Fax: 01759 372513

**Claire's Sugarcraft**
Norfolk House Yard
St Nicholas Street
Diss, Norfolk
IP22 4LB
Tel: 01379 650082

**Confectionary Supplies**
31 Lower Cathedral Road
Cardif CF11 7LU
Tel: 02920 372161

**Culpitt Ltd**
Jubilee Industrial Estate
Ashington
Northumberland NE63 8UQ
Tel: 01670 814545
Fax: 01670 815248
www.culpitt.com

**Fine Cut Sugarcraft Products**
Workshop 2
Old Stable Block
Holme Pierrepont Hall
Holme Pierrepont
Nottingham NG12 2LD
Tel/fax: 01159 334349

**Holly Products**
Holly Cottage
Hassell Green
Cheshire CW11 4YA
Tel/fax: 01270 761403

**Kit Box**
1 Fernlea Gardens
Easton in Gordano
Bristol BS20 0JF
Tel/fax: 01275 374557

**Orchard Products**
51 Hallyburton Road
Hove
East Sussex BN3 7GP
Tel: 01273 919418

**PME/Knights Bridge Bakeware Centre Ltd**
Chadwell Heath Lane
Romford
Essex RM6 4NP
Tel: 020 8590 5959
Fax: 020 8590 7373
www.cakedecoration.co.uk

**Renshaw Scott Ltd**
Crown Street
Liverpool L8 7RF
Tel: 0870 870 6954
Fax: 0870 870 6955
www.renshawscott.co.uk or
www.supercook.co.uk

**Squires Kitchen (Great Impressions)**
Squires House
3 Waverley Lane
Farnham
Surrey GU9 8BB
Tel: 0845 2255 671
www.squires-group.co.uk

**Sugar City**
78 Battle Road
St Leonards-on-Sea
E Sussex TN37 7AG
Tel: 01424 432448
Fax: 01424 421359
www.sugarcity.co.uk

**Tinkertech Two**
40 Langdon Road
Parkstone, Poole
Dorset BN14 9EH
Tel: 01202 738 049

## NEW ZEALAND

**Decor Cakes**
Victoria Arcade
435 Great South Road
Otahuhu
Auckland
Tel: (09) 276 6676

**Milly's Kitchen Shop**
273 Ponsonby Road
Ponsonby
Auckland
Tel: (09) 376 1550

**Spotlight**
(branches throughout NZ)
Wairau Park
19 Link Drive
Glenfield, Auckland
Tel: (09) 444 0220
www.spotlightonline.co.nz

## SOUTH AFRICA

**Confectionery Extravaganza**
Shop 48, Flora Centre
Ontdekkers Road
Florida, West Rand 1724
Johannesburg
Tel: (011) 672 4766

**Jem Cutters**
128 Crompton Street
Pinetown 3610
Durban
Tel: (031) 701 1431
Fax: (031) 701 0559

## AUSTRALIA

**Cake Art Supplies**
Kiora Mall
Shop 26 Kora Road
Miranda
NSW 2228
Tel: (02) 9540 3483

**Cake and Icing Centre**
651 Samford Road
Mitchelton
Queensland 4053
Tel: (07) 3355 3443

# index

# acknowledgments

I would like to thank Vida, without whose help and support this book would never have been finished. Andrew, for all his support and for cooking me such lovely dinners! Debs for transferring all my scribblings onto the computer. Alison Proctor, for letting me use her ideas for the freesia, viola and cyclamen. My parents for their endless support and encouragement, especially Mum as she spent many hours looking after the shop while I was writing and making flowers. Alastair, who looked after the shop.

I would also like to thank Rosemary Wilkinson and Clare Sayer at New Holland for asking me to write the book and Shona Wood for creating some lovely photographs.